THE MAKING OF
THE HOLISTIC WOMAN

A LIFESTYLE GUIDE TO ACHIEVING PHYSICAL, MENTAL AND SPIRITUAL WELLBEING FOR THE MODERN WOMAN

OLIVIA 'MCOLIVIA' UCHECHUKWU

OLIVIA "MCOLIVA" UCHECHUKWU

THE MAKING OF THE HOLISTIC WOMAN:
A LIFESTYLE GUIDE TO ACHIEVING PHYSICAL, MENTAL AND SPIRITUAL WELLBEING FOR THE MODERN WOMAN
Copyright ©2021 by **OLIVIA 'MCOLIVIA' UCHECHUKWU**

ISBN: 979-8457375581

Published in Nigeria by

Naphtali Publishers
(a division of Rayany Enterprise)
60, Olatunde Close, Agidingbi, Ikeja, Lagos.
Tel: 2348131978457, 2348136028328

Email: publish@naphtali.com.ng
Website: www.naphtali.com.ng

FOREWARD

I got to know Olivia Uchechukwu (McOlivia) through Facebook in 2015 and we became good friends. Our friendship led to her managing my Nigerian music promotion campaign for me. We shared ideas on many issues and I assisted her with her McOlivia Foundation here in the USA.

Having read and reviewed her book, "The Making of a Holistic Woman", I would encourage everyone male and female who truly wants to make a difference in their lives and in the world to read this great work. This book "The Making of a Holistic Woman", contains great words of advice, research, statistics and knowledge on how to be a better and balanced woman. This book also has a unique style of combining storytelling with information giving as it explains the 'what', the 'who', the 'where', the 'why' and the 'how' of becoming a great woman in our world today.

I am writing this foreword not only because I was asked to but because I learnt a lot from reading this work. I applaud this work because it gives factual and concrete examples backed by scholarly research, applies to all women in the world and will definitely make a big difference in the lives of all who read it.

Fr. Fidelis Omeaku (RevFICO)

OLIVIA "MCOLIVA" UCHECHUKWU

DEDICATION

To two of the most amazing women in my life; my mother, Fidelia Ifesinachi Onyia and my daughter, Chukwumeli November Uchechukwu.

ACKNOWLEDGEMENT

Firstly, I would like to acknowledge the inspiration and direction of the Holy Spirit from whom all wisdom for this project flows. Thank God for his love and grace that has kept me alive and in good health to conceive, begin and finish this book.

A big thank you to my publisher, Naphtali Books, who worked with me from start to set my book outline and timeline and continued to supervise my writing till it was complete. Thank you to my Publicity and Distribution managers, Book House Nigeria, my shoot production team for photographs contained in this book. The fashion contributors like Emara, Geraldine Apparels, Beryl Hairs and Raylivia, for the outfits for this book. And thank you to Studio Bok, for my cover design. As well as Savvy gardens, I AM FIT Gym and MMB Spa for their collaboration. Appreciation goes to all my Advanced Readers on this book, Psychologist and Emotional health therapist, Eberechukwu Onah, Pastor Chukwuemeka Nwokike and my UK based Pastry chef and yoga enthusiast who chose to stay anonymous.

I'm grateful to the passionate involvement of Rev. Fr. Fidelis Omeaku (RevFICO) that kept me on the course throughout the process.

Thank you to my parents, Engr. Ferdinand Okey Onyia and Mrs Fidelia Ifesinachi Onyia, who have made me into the young queen that I am today. And to my siblings, Ada, Dera, Dessy and Vivian.

My deepest gratitude goes to my husband and editor, Ray Anyasi. And of course thank you to my sweet mum-in-law, Deaconess Philomena Onyefuose Anyasi, whose love and stories helped me make up my mind to write. Thank you to my precious daughter, my cute Miss November Chukwumeli. The kindest, most thoughtful and most patient two year old ever.

And to all my friends and every woman whose life has inspired my own in no small way, Thank you!

Table of Contents

CHAPTER I

INTRODUCTION

As a little girl, I always dreamed of being a writer someday. The more I wrote poems and short stories, the more I wanted to publish and share my outlook on life. I became a teenager and the voice of the little girl waned as the influence of my immediate environment became a predominant narrator in my life's stories.

As a young adult, I started to stumble through life and inadvertently manifest the realities of my perceptions.

And then I became a woman, and suddenly everything changed. I realized that it wasn't just enough to keep on dreaming. It was finally time to wake up and live my dreams. And I was awoken by the loud realities of the Woman's world today.

I had come to a place where the women around me were fast rising the corporate ladder and taking their place on the global market scene. At the same time some of these women were also becoming wives, and mothers and somehow in the excitement of the journey before us, we were slowly beginning to forget the little girl that we all once were and the simple pleasures we enjoyed in everyday living. Such as a warm smile from a loved one, or a hot plate of our favorite meal or even a simple run with friends in the neighborhood. I also came to see the pain in the eyes of the women around me who didn't dare reach for their dreams because they had taken the title of wife and mother and hung it like a noose around their necks and so they were too afraid to do anything because they were held by leashes of their own imaginations.

So I took time off from my own work and started to ask myself questions I should have answered years ago. How did we get here as women? Why are we becoming more economically relevant but less and less satisfied? Why do we ever self-sabotage? And how can we reclaim our lives in such a way that we cast depression and anxiety far away from our door post? How can the modern woman begin to enjoy her life, irrespective of her predicaments, whether she is single or in a relationship, rich or poor, old or young, and irrespective of her past and the path she has chosen for her life?

There was no better place to begin the search for these answers than my very own life and experiences. At 24, I had toured Africa as a stand-up comedienne in the company of other comedy legends like Klint De Drunk, I had established myself and flourished in a career as a prime time radio and TV host, I had become a general manager for a radio station. At 28, I had established my charity foundation and organized three editions of the Everybody Deserves a Merry Christmas project across major African cities, I had produced and hosted a show on a major cable network, Africa Magic, I had hosted notable live shows, conferences and carnivals for multinationals in front of tens of thousands of live guests and even world leaders in attendance, I had started my production company which began shooting our own multi-million Naira reality TV show, my restaurant business was booming, delivering meals to clients in Lagos, Abuja, Enugu and Europe.

All was well and good, or so I thought. I was excelling in my career as a woman and I had a loving husband. And then I became a mother. And a new dawn began.

Motherhood put such great pressure on me to manifest the highest level of my true self. I was forced to truly consider the quality of life that I was going to impart to my darling daughter whom I love with all my heart. What will I teach her about life? How will I be sure that she grows up happy and enjoys the best quality of life possible? What would her priorities be? I wanted to do right by her so much. And in raising a girl-child, I found myself again. Watching her grow before my eyes made me appreciate the miracle that is our life as women. And to take a closer look at my body, which had borne this beautiful miracle. We often judge our bodies at different times but even more harshly after we bring forth life, focusing more on the changes we undergo rather than on the beautiful stories told by our stretch marks and dark spots. For me, motherhood has and always will be a beautiful blessing, even with all the trials it presents.

But in all my understanding and appreciation of my physical body, alas, I was already struggling. I was struggling to catch my breath as I juggled my roles as business woman, role model, wife and now mother. And in my struggle, I forgot the most important person I needed to be always, a WOMAN.

And so I made the most classic mistake in the books, I began to betray my basic needs as a woman in my bid to be who I thought everybody else needed me to be. An occasional skipping a meal to keep in shape or indulging junks because I didn't plan better, or delaying bedtime to run one more errand or missing a morning run because the outdoors didn't feel safe enough, and then judging myself for not being the Superwoman I allowed others trick me into thinking that I was.

It wasn't until I had my second miscarriage that my already threatened Pandora's box burst wide open and I was finally forced to look at myself in the mirror. And the woman that looked back at me had so much hurt in her eyes from all the pain of the past amplified by my most recent trials. Pain from the ones who had betrayed me, and from the times I had betrayed myself every time I did not prioritize my self care.

In this time, for the first time in my life, I stopped being strong, stopped resisting and stopped running and finally let all the raw emotions hit me from every corner. Painful and intense blows that felt like my heart was ripped out from within me. My carefree approach to life became tainted as I had been faced with a few struggles with my identity. This was precipitated in no small way by memories of a near sexual abuse that resulted in a physical beating when I tried to speak up about it and then a robbery leading to an abduction that coded fear and anxiety into the blueprint of my existential instincts. These, accompanied by other unpleasant events of my young adult life, had haunted my subconscious and silently triggered a fast advancing psychological metamorphoses of a personality I detested, yet dreaded to confront.

For the first time, I chose to confront my past and heal myself and the relationships in my life. I wanted to live and to live free of all struggle, shame and pain.

I decided to put my house in order. I realized at this point that I was the biggest hero in my own life story and so I had to show up for myself and step away from every delusion of blame and entitlement. The job of living a holistic lifestyle with good health in spirit, soul and body was all mine. As I explored this discovery, I found true joy and happiness that transcended any outward occurrences and lived safely within me.

In that beautiful moment, frozen forever in history, I chose to love myself and to take care of myself. I made peace with everything and everyone in my past, and by the mercies of God, I was able to shake off the anxiety and fear that had slowly crept in with every unresolved traumas and past challenges and to step fully into the light and as I looked in the mirror again, I could recognize who I was once more. Behold, Woman!

My physical, mental, social, financial and emotional health had been plugged back into fertile ground, and I began to blossom again. It was my mother whose voice rang loud as she answered my question of "why me?" with "why not you?". Her years as an English Literature teacher had made her thoroughly skilled in the use of probing queries to answer life's difficult questions and I found her outlook on taking personal responsibility for one's self refreshing. It drew me back to a place where I woke up each morning desiring to pursue a life of Holistic Living where taking care of my own self and getting the appropriate nutrition, hygiene, rest and relationships mattered more in my effective work as a functional member of society.

In all, it was my little daughter that taught me to show up for myself every day. In her cute and adorable way, she would always smile and remind me to eat when I feed her, to take a bath when I bathe her, to brush my hair when I brushed hers, and to get a massage when I massaged her. It was taking care of my daughter that reminded me to take care of me always. And even as I pursue a meaningful career, never to lose sight of my self care and the things that truly matter.

As a mother, wife, sister, daughter and girlfriend, it has finally dawned on me that our path as women has been divinely orchestrated in a way that not only adds color to our world but should colour our own individual experiences in ways that only rainbows dare. It is in this discovery of the balance between the woman and her world that I have finally arrived at a place of awareness, where the realities of my own existence finally outweigh the voices of my perception. And in this place, there are no limitations and the possibilities are endless.

As I look inward again, I draw from my own life experiences and return to the little girl who dreamed dreams and sought only to interpret her dreams. And those dreams are simple; to share my life in a way that empowers the next woman to reach into her innermost heart and begin to manifest her full potential. This is why Chapter 2 begins by addressing our perceptions as women, with a view to get to the root of our thought process understanding fully well that our thoughts form our words which in turn become our actions and our actions become our habits and our habits rule our everyday life.

I know that for myself and for every woman to begin to make the right choices concerning her nutrition, exercise, work, rest and relaxation as well as the relationships she surrounds herself with, she must first come to a place where she first adjusts her mindset and begins to take personal responsibility for her health and well being. If we continue to blame our background, past relationships and those who have hurt us in the past for the choices we make today, then we may never truly take back the control of our lives from them.

Now I acknowledge that this change is not easy and this is why I have taken the time to walk with you in this journey through the pages of this book. From the state of your mental well being to factors that strengthen the physical, spiritual, emotional, financial and social health of a holistic woman. It is in the elements of the thoughts we entertain, the choice of food we eat, the exercise we engage in, the quality of rest and relaxation we allow ourselves, the positive energy we harvest from the relationships we nurture around us, the deliberate and strategic thoughts we give to managing our financial resources, and most importantly, the wisdom with which we handle the subject of our spirituality.

I address all these with my most painstaking effort at simplicity and clarity. I do this, drawing from a rich pool of universal, yet scarcely contemplated knowledge, thoughtfully critiqued along the rationale of the logical walls that the wells of my lived experiences agreeably accepts.

My hope is that, as you read this book, there will be an awakening for you and you can begin to retrace your steps and align completely to the fullness of the power available to you. You can be the best wife or mother possible, and the best sister or friend ever, and the best colleague or mentor, as well as the most financially stable woman in your generation. Most Importantly, you can have peace inside of you, unperturbed by the troubles of life, whoever you choose to be and wherever life leads you.

Reach for it, be the holistic Woman that you know you were born to be.

We're in this together, *QUEEN*.

The world is ready for you and so are you.
Let the journey begin.
Sincerely,
Olivia 'McOlivia' Uchechukwu,
Wife, Mother, Daughter, Sister, Friend,
WOMAN!

CHAPTER 2
PERCEPTIONS

Buogo is an elegant young lady who works a 9-5 job and runs a packaging on the side. As a single lady, she enjoys the company of her girlfriends, most of whom have settled into marriage and become mothers over the years.

Her best friend Pamela, lives a carefree life and would often go dancing alone and this bothered Buogo because Pam is married and in her opinion, have absolutely no business going dancing alone. She could never wrap her head round a married woman *flexing life* at what she considers the expense of her family. But she has grown tired of the endless fights between them whenever she tries to *counsel's* her about what it means to be responsibly married. It hurt so much whenever the conversation ends up on the topic of her singleness. As Pam would so often put it, she is single to stupor. And not because she doesn't have any suitors.

They have been best friends since high school and so, even though their values have slightly changed, their bond of friendship remains intact. It is for this reason that Buogo elected to babysit for Pam whenever she goes dancing just so her husband wouldn't be upset. And it is also for this reason that she never really finds the time to hang out with her many prospective suitors and give her own love-life a fighting chance.

Most of her free time are spent trying to assist her many friends who seem to always have one problem or the other whenever she comes around. She is the most dependable lady in their circle of friends, the ever available miss Fix-it.

Deep inside, she is hurting and would sometimes cry herself to sleep because it seems like the more she gives herself, the more people take and take and take. She can't quite get it to stop and even as kind and well meaning as she figures she is, there are still some persons who wouldn't stop taking advantage of her kindness, like her siblings who never keep in touch no matter how many times she checks up on them, some of her colleagues who think she's a snob, her friends who don't promote her side hustle and her romantic interests who sometimes end up leaving her for the most ridiculous excuses.

And now that Pam has given birth to twins, she wonders how she is going to combine her 9-5 job with her business and the unpaid babysitting of 3 children who never seem to be full no matter how many bottles of breast milk Pam expresses and stores in the fridge against her many nights out. For all of her shortcomings, her *bestie* is a good mother, and has committed to exclusively breastfeeding her children for their first 6 months. In Buogo's books, that is the greatest show of love and commitment a mother could give her babies.

She is awake again this night, trying to seal all the orders from her growing client base overnight. She is grateful for the massive growth her business have recorded in just 2 years of opening shop. Her finances are finally getting better, and if only the people around her would stop being so clueless and aloof, her life would be perfect.

As the sealing machine gives off a small smoke while sealing the 8th bag of products, Buogo wonders how long it would take her to fix them all and get them to finally like her for who she really is.

But it was easy to suspect that even Buogo have yet to ask the question, who am I really?

****

The issue of personal identity is one that I believe is at the core of most of life's drama. Who I am deep within me determines my outlook on life and shapes my expectations and experiences. But I have heard some people I respect say severally that perception is stronger than reality. As much as I resisted that insinuation/assertion in the beginning, time has proven how powerful perception can be.

> **Personal identity is who I see myself to be. It is made up of my values, behavior, culture, etc. it is my vision of myself.**
>
> **On the other hand, perception is the lens that helps my vision of myself.**

If you are the daughter of a king and you don't consider yourself as such, you will expect to be treated as less than royalty and perpetually attract same. Your decisions will be shaped by your perception of yourself.

I've met some ladies who exude such level of confidence that you would find it hard to refuse them anything they ask. Sometimes they don't have any material thing to justify the way they carry themselves. They carry on as though they have everything working out for them and even in the face of likely embarrassment, they stay classy and never lose their cool. In the past, I used to be drawn to such women and just look upon them in awe. They seemed untouchable and completely unperturbed, like Divas and Queens. I have a few of them as friends and work with a few. Among these women, I had identified those who I believed were snobs and the ones who I was sure had inferiority complexes. And so, I treated each person as I thought they deserved to be treated based on my perception of them.

Sometimes someone would move from being an acquaintance to a friend and then after a few months of intense friendship, I would disqualify them and move them back to the outer circle. And vice-versa. Maybe they were getting too close or they were too selfish or too demanding or too manipulative or too nice. But as the cycle continued, I realized that I didn't have stability in my relationships and so I decided to change strategy because I desired more stability and wanted to enjoy genuine human connections found in friendship. Instead of thinking about others, I started to look inward and wonder what it was about me that made it difficult to maintain stable relationships. And that was a turning point in my relationships.

So here are some things I discovered were defining my perceptions and influencing my life choices and experiences. And the more I meditated on these things and discussed it with others, I realized it was the same things that were affecting most other people in their everyday life. The issue of Personal Identity influences our level of Self confidence/belief/esteem, and is a sum total of our cultural identity, family background, and peer influence (this includes social media influence).

2.1 SELF CONFIDENCE/SELF ESTEEM /SELF BELIEF

I believe that a confident woman is someone who, irrespective of her age, social status, or achievement, is sure of herself and wears her scars and crowns proudly. She flaunts her strengths, not in an arrogant way, but in an assertive manner that exudes grace and class. She is honest with herself on the areas of her weaknesses, but this knowledge empowers rather than diminishes her, because she is a constantly evolving being. Confidence has nothing to do with feeling superior or inferior to others. It is a quiet inner knowledge that you're enough. You are kind enough to say Yes to the things that you can do but you also love yourself enough to say NO to the things that you cannot do.

> **Self esteem is the worth that one places on him/herself based on their personal evaluation of self.**

A woman who has a high sense of self worth, has a healthy self esteem. And this shows in the way she relates with her family, friends, colleagues and especially with herself. I believe some persons have mastered the art of faking confidence, where they appear confident but deep within they are afraid and shaking at their prevailing circumstance. You can appear confident without having a healthy self esteem. In our society today, there is a heightened dependence on material things to boost one's confidence. But no matter how many expensive shoes and jewelry a woman owns, or the brand of makeup and lingerie she wears, or the calibre of men she dates, or even the part of the world she lives in and the number of cars and houses she owns, she may never really feel whole inside if she has a low self-image and worth. It is easy to lie to the audience and pretend like you are confident in public, hiding behind your designer glasses that shield everybody from looking into your eyes which can be the window to your soul. But it is almost impossible to lie to yourself when you're alone at night, having washed off the makeup and the mask you wear daily, that overwhelming feeling of emptiness and worthlessness comes from a place of being broken and not knowing how to heal the wounds in your heart and soul.

There was a time in my life when I was too uncomfortable to go anywhere without Make up. Even for casual runs like going to the bank or the farmer's market, I had to put on at least loose powder, draw on brows & wear lip gloss. It had started innocently in high school where almost all the girls wore colored lip gloss in a bid to glow and impress our teenage crushes. Granted, I went to school in a dry clime, and during the harmattan season, lip gloss and balms were essential to keep one's lips from cracking. But a number of us found the harmattan a worthy excuse to wear light make up, which were banned, at the time. We were just teenagers *catching cruise* and we got away with it.

Then I went on to university and would spend a large amount of time putting on makeup and sometimes appearing late to class. I remember one of my roommates in my first year at the University of Nigeria, Nsukka, who took it upon herself to harass me for wearing makeup to class. She was almost sure I would give up make up after just one semester facing the rigour of THE DEN, as my school was called. I laugh when I wonder what she would have said if she saw me at my convocation ceremony, wearing my first full face of makeup. I had graduated from putting on makeup by myself to having an expert makeup artiste do it for me and so I wore my first professional make up on the day of my convocation.

Then I got a job as a TV presenter, and it became mandatory for me to wear makeup as I was required to look flawless on TV. I had to find a Makeup artist, who was really gracious and would come to our TV station every day to make me up. With time, I couldn't keep up with her payments because it was costing me a lot to pay her from my own salary and at this time my employers were gracious enough to intervene and have one of our production staff who was a Make Up artiste on the side volunteer to keep me flawless on TV.

When I resigned that job, it occurred to me how attached to *face-beats* I had become. I was rarely seen without Make Up and would rush to put on light make up in the restroom whenever I came to work, even when I wouldn't be on set for the day. It was a tough road deprogramming myself and getting back to thoroughly loving my natural face. But I did it eventually.

I recovered so well that I'd only wear makeup if I have to go on stage (as an event host) or go on TV as a presenter.

Plot twist, one day, my Make Up Artiste was running late & it was Day three of Lagos Comic Con, an international event I was hosting, I didn't waste any moment to climb that stage without any make up & host the event beautifully.

Another time, I was producing a wedding event for my TV series, The Real of Bridesmaids of Africa, and I had planned a surprise for the bride so I was all over the place. My Make Up artiste had to chase me around just to draw on my eyebrows. It wasn't until we were done with that day's production that it occurred to me that I had gone on air without wearing full make up and had done a flawless job.

I loved the feeling of freedom that came with being me and basking in the imperfections that make me a truly remarkable and unique individual. Every quirky character, freckle and out-of-place dot, a deliberate design by an undisputed master creator in the impeccable work of Art called Me.

Sometimes I just ponder on how much conditioning we're exposed to as a people and especially as women. We are made to desire seemingly perfect body figures, flawless skin, the perfect dentition, unimaginable hair lengths, impossible accents, impractical butt sizes etc.

I love to play dress up & look nice. I believe that the art of being fascinating is a mesmerizing tool for a woman; which is why I make a conscious and intentional effort to smell and look good. But now, I have enough common sense to realize that the moment I go from enjoying these adjustments to feeling like I desperately need them to be complete, whole or enough, then I am giving in to social conditioning and allowing peer pressure, sponsored campaigns and advertising to best me. And I absolutely do not want to be played like that.

We may need to stop chasing perfection and acknowledge that there is a bit of insecurity in every one of us, and that is just alright.

I think that if we identify it and are honest enough to acknowledge it, its powers over us begin to wane notably. And in that place of awareness and honesty, we are able to ask ourselves the questions that really matter. Why do I feel the need to conform to society's expectations of a woman? Why am I eager to please everyone even at my own detriment? Why am I so stressed working so hard just to afford the things that do not really matter to me? Why do I keep getting and getting and getting without ever feeling enough? Why am I so uncomfortable with how I look, what I do, where I'm from and who I am? Why do I feel so empty sometimes?

I can write about this so clearly and so intensely because it is a state where I lived in for so many years before I was rescued. My healing began when I consciously began to ask myself these important questions. I read so many different books and attended women conferences and listened to audio messages genuinely seeking answers to why my self esteem was so brittle and my confidence such a brave effort. To do the work I do in the way that I do it, with whom I do it, where I do it and in the time that I do it, a healthy self esteem and confidence are non-negotiable. So for me, wholeness was a matter of personal and professional urgency. And what I found to be at the heart of the battle was that my Personal Identity was scarred. I had no real sense of who I am and I depended on everybody else to define me. In my journey of self-discovery, I realized there are some factors that contributed to most of my issues with low self esteem and I find the same to be true with most people I have met who suffer the same fate. Issues surrounding family background, peer influence, and cultural identity contribute intensely to produce feelings that result in experiences of shame, pride, greed, jealousy, envy, and guilt which are all manifestations of an unhealthy self esteem. Interestingly, I found that my perceptions of my family background, peer influence and cultural identity were just instruments I was using to self sabotage. In reality, my perceptions were simply that. Perceptions.

It is so easy to miss it and yet I felt so silly when I finally realized that my Personal Identity and Self Esteem can be healthy irrespective of my past, present or future. This is one of the realizations that started me on my journey to freedom. And I hope that it will help you in some ways too.

Cultural Identity

We live in interesting times, where we have been able to successfully bridge the gap between tribes and continents, thanks to the Internet. However, I think that as technologically advanced as we have become as women, we are still largely influenced by our place of origin. Yes, we travel and live far away from our place of birth and yes, we have cut off our *village people*, but truly our cultural identity is most likely embedded deeply in our DNA. There has been studies recently that show that who we are, at our core, can be a reflection of the predominant culture and values of where we come from. Take for instance, the constant comparison between the Igbos of South Eastern

Nigeria and the Jews, many people allege that the two nations must have been one at some point in history because of similarities in their traditional practices like the circumcision of male children eight days after birth, identification of certain foods as **unclean** and unfit for consumption, and mourning the dead for seven days etc. Some anthropologists claim that the Igbos were practicing these customs before their exposure to the Bible and Christian missionaries.

According to a once trending CNN article, Daniel Lis, a researcher on Jewish identification among the Igbo from the Institute for Jewish Studies, University of Basel, Switzerland, says, there has been a clear continuity of Jewish identity among the Igbo. It's not just something that happened yesterday.

In 2018, I did a feature on the Alaba International Market in Lagos, West Africa, to highlight the Apprenticeship system of the Igbos known popularly as *Igba boy*, interviewing the key players in this entrepreneurship system. An entrepreneur, more commonly referred to as *Oga*, brings a young boy of common origins, to live with him, work with him and understudy him as an apprentice, with view of providing him capital and business mentorship for his own business after the agreed duration of service. During the apprenticeship training period, technical, management and interpersonal skills like market research, forecasting, book keeping, human relations, communication and negotiation, as well as diversification and business scaling are learned. The research was an episode of the Ebe Ngoli show, aired on Africa Magic Igbo. As a people, it would seem that entrepreneurship is largely ingrained in an Igbo woman's DNA and I have always found it fascinating, being a serial entrepreneur myself. It wasn't until I got married and started to relate closely with my husband's people that I caught a close glimpse of the sharp contrast between my culture and his own and how it influenced my behavior different from his.

Apart from the speculations of Jewish origin as an explanation of the entrepreneurial nature of the Igbos, I discovered that the The Nigerian Civil War, fought between 1967 and 1970 left a huge mark on the Igbos as a people. Academic, financial and social integration back into the Nigerian system as well as continued sustenance was met with a wall. For starters, Nigerian Government policies made sure that the richest Igbo man at that time had nothing more than 20 Pounds, No Igbo child had been to school in those three years, and the Igbo professional was viewed with suspicion in his Nigerian workplace. One can understand how this reality would drive the Igbos into an ambitious overdrive to work, work, and achieve.

My mother-in-law is a lovely woman who I have enjoyed many interesting conversations with over cocoa tea, and it is from her that I learned that my husband's Town of Issele-Mkpitime in Delta state did not experience the war.

My husband, my mother-in-law and I had that conversation one regular evening in my family house and it was as though my marriage and my husband made so much sense in that moment. You see, my husband is just as keen on rest as he is on work and it didn't make sense to me why he would take things as easy as he did sometimes, because I had an inexplicable desire to achieve all the time, which is generally a good thing, but I realized I may have been caught in over-drive once in a while in my entrepreneurship journey because of my cultural identity. I am from a generation of doers. It was on that day that I realized that even though I was not a part of the war, its effects had subconsciously trickled down from the generations before me and I had acquired some behaviours, both good and bad, from my ancestors who experienced the war. So, I made my peace with my history and from then on, began to consciously manifest only the aspects of my cultural identity that resonate with my present realities.

I am now deliberate to join my husband in an afternoon nap if my body feels tired, because there is no imminent war looming, and nobody is coming to take away the fruit of my hard work in the blink of an eye. I learned to really rest and began to deliberately pamper myself at every given opportunity. The result is that I am less anxious than I used to be, because I am less stressed or overworked. I used to shy away from my father's stories of our family history but now I listen with rapt attention, because in understanding where I'm from, I have begun to understand who I am and why I do what I do and therefore get closer to wholeness as a woman.

I am proud to come from a tribe of relentless achievers, who are known to thrive and excel in any country or situation we find ourselves. But now, even as I excel in my work, I am deliberate about rest and relaxation. Knowledge of my cultural identity is not an excuse to wallow in self pity but is empowering me to live my best life, as a doer and achiever who prioritizes rest and relaxation. In my home, I am doing my best to create an environment for my daughter to have a childhood highlighted by many happy moments of rest and relaxation. I share more on Work, as well as rest and relaxation in Chapters 4 and 5 of this book.

As women, we must be deliberate about rest and relaxation because our body does wonders from the age of puberty till menopause, and from our monthly menstrual cycle to childbirth, we give a lot of ourselves and so we definitely need to rest from time to time. For you, it may not be your attitude towards work and rest that your cultural identity affects, but I believe you may be better served if you can find out what aspects of yourself is consistent with your place of origin, and decide for yourself if you like the effect on you or not. That way, you can embrace what works and do your best to adjust the aspects that affect you negatively.

Another apt example is present in the cultural identity of the Ashanti women of Ghana. In 2016, I directed a stage play at the President Barack Obama's Young African Leaders Initiative program. The play was based on the story of Queen Mother Nana Yaa Asantewaa, who led an army of 5,000 in The Ashanti-British War of the Golden Stool. She was the first and only woman in Asante history chosen by a number of regional Asante kings to be the war-leader of the Asante fighting force in such a historically deciding war.

Yaa Asantewaa's dream for an Asante free of British rule was realized on 6 March 1957, when the Asante protectorate gained independence as part of Ghana. Ghana was the first African nation in Sub-Saharan Africa to achieve this feat.

I find her story so inspiring and it made sense that the few Ashanti ladies I interacted with in my time in Ghana seemed quite bold and daring. I guess her story would have had a big impact on them.

In my Igbo culture, practices like the use of kitchen stools (oche ntukwu) and bathing stools foster mindfulness which help to curb anxiety. I smile when I think of this because it wasn't until I brought back stools to my bathrooms and kitchens to help me take things easy and rest systemically that I realized the wisdom of my ancestors. Today, psychology preaches mindfulness as a way to mitigate anxiety but I am proud that the women of my tribe had long figured out this life hack of taking things easy by sitting down while working amidst friendly conversation.

Family Background

Different authors and storytellers have drawn interesting parallels on the lives of the Haves and the Have-nots, and the impact of economic status on the sense of self worth a child draws from their immediate family. Some have even gone on to measure the extent of damage that can be done when a child grows up in a dysfunctional home where the parents are either separated, divorced, or experiencing some form of marital crisis.

Verbal abuse, physical abuse and even emotional abuse have all been quoted as culprits, in instances where an adult exhibits repulsive behavior. We excuse it as, she sleeps around because she seeks validation from men since she had an absentee father, or he beats his wife because he has a fragile ego or his own father used to beat his mother or he embezzles public funds because he was poor growing up and he doesn't want his generation to experience poverty ever again. Every day, we see the chaos and mayhem in our personal lives and society and the pain in our neighbor's eyes and it seems like we are helpless, but I like to think that there is a way out.

I have seen and heard about people who came from the most unlikely and unfavorable family backgrounds rise above every doubt in their head and become a success story. I have interviewed big personalities on VVIP Red carpets who came from nothing and became something against all odds. I have also interviewed individuals on my radio and TV shows who come from the most unlikely family backgrounds and turned out to be a blessing to their family and society rather than reenact the mayhem they experienced in their own past. And so I know, that although family backgrounds can be a great influence in one's life, it is not the ultimate determinant of success and failure. Your childhood could have been terrible, but your children do not have to go through the same things you experienced too. And you may have been unloved and abused growing up, but it is now time to turn the tides in your own favor. In Chapter 8 of this book, I did my best to discuss the dynamics of family relationships, in a way that instead of allowing our past to continue to cripple our present and malign the future, we can even attempt to heal ourselves from family troubles and mend our relationships enough to enjoy our present and hope for a better future. It sounds easier said than done, but the least we can do is try.

Peer Influence

Growing up, I watched my mother and her peers convene for the annual August Meeting in the village, which is a prevalent culture in the Eastern part of Nigeria where I come from. I absolutely love the potentials for friendship and sisterhood that I saw in those meetings, but they were sometimes hijacked by the natural penchant for some of the women to show off social and financial status in a way that made some of the other women, who were insecure, crawl into their own shells. I sincerely yearn for such traditions to be resurrected and vibrant in our time, because of some of the good I reckon it did for the women, but sadly, it continues to wane and wane into oblivion.

In our world of social media, perceptions have spiraled out of control with the *fake-it-till-you-make-it* vibe that has overtaken many of us as women. Even the persons who have nothing to gain by faking it are drawn into an endless web of self-deceit. There are influencers who brands pay as part of their marketing campaign to look a certain way on social media, in order to propagate a narrative for their business growth. So, your *idol* comes on social media to post a new type of hairstyle or a new car or her latest piercing and suddenly you lose all home training and your personal contentment jumps out the window.

As a PR professional, I have been privileged to work with a few businesses on their branding campaigns. It has given me a humble outlook on the things I see on the Internet. From marketing, to brand positioning, and algorithms, most things we see online is a manifestation of what advertisers wish to propagate to improve their market share and maximize profits. So brand influencers are empowered to sell a narrative and influence their audience to buy that narrative and women who have absolutely no business with the narrative jump on and begin to bend over backwards to embrace what is at best an illusion. There are certain products for certain people. We must not all wear waist trainers and stiletto heels. Our decisions should be fuelled by our personal needs, and not glamorous advertising. But do we even understand what our basic needs are? Do we even remember to eat at the right time, have a bath, take a deep breath, visit our loved ones, and sleep when we're tired? Are the basic necessities of life fuelling our work, lifestyle and everyday choices? Or are we moved about by the latest Instagram post of our *faves* who live thousands of miles away from us and are oblivious of our existence?

I hear that brands are moving over to *micro-influencers* these days as more people discover the cleverness of influencer-marketing and develop increased resistance towards big influencers whose near-perfect lifestyles have become obvious advertising baits. It would be interesting to see how we respond when our friends who have 100 followers on Instagram begin to suddenly afford things that leave us shocked because these are people we know and live with. If we understand that social media is a virtual make-belief world and approach it with a level of sanity, then our own physical realities would begin to approach true happiness and peace. The fact that your neighbor who used to ask you for salt now suddenly posts photos in the most luxurious hotels and exotic cars and vacation hotspots shouldn't cause you to lose sleep and focus, she may simply be influencing for a hotel or car company, or be on a sponsored vacation for a travel agency. These are all valid jobs that people do in our world today. And do not go spreading lies that she is a person of loose morals, you just need to reset your brain and open your mind and eliminate all judgment and stop exposing yourself to unnecessary anxiety. If you can't stand the *going-ons* on the Internet, please take a break for as long as you need and return when and if-ever you're ready. We're in the Tech age, know this and know peace. And just be kind to yourself and allow yourself room to grow, as organically as possible, without comparing yourself to others so much.

In conclusion, it is important that we lay this foundation first before continuing into the next chapters of this book, because I realize that while some people already have a healthy sense of self, some others may not be so fortunate.

> *So my hope is that as we adjust our perceptions and bring it closer to our reality, we will be a lot more honest with ourselves and kinder with our progress in a way that makes our journey towards holistic living more enjoyable, and less of a judgmental struggle.*

Once we have acknowledged and adjusted our sense of Personal Identity to a frequency where we stop allowing excuses and the past to cripple us, but instead decide to maximize the best aspects of our cultural and family backgrounds as well as our peer relationships, then I am convinced that we just might be ready for the next phase.

So let us journey on to explore ways to eat right, get adequate rest and relaxation, exercise, as well as flourish in our work and spiritual path. If the goal is to live right, enjoy good health and wealth, and still be available to love and be loved, then we better get moving.

Let's go ladies!

> *Excuse me,*
> *I don't know you.*
> *Excuse me,*
> *I can't see you.*
> *My worth is in me,*
> *Not in your head.*
> *My value is my burden,*
> *Release yourself.*
> *Go your way, I'd go mine.*
> *I can't see you,*
> *Excuse me.*

Excuse Me - **Ray Anyasi**

CHAPTER 3
NUTRITION

When the car sped out the driveway, the loud whistle of the trees over the tinted window of the SUV was proof that the city had gone to sleep. Buogo knew that to make it to the bakery in time, she may have to break one or two traffic laws, but that was the least of her worries. LASTMA has gone to sleep, she hoped, as she doubled down on the gas pedal, flying straight into the busy Lagos traffic, and then slowing down almost to a halt as the heavy traffic weighed on her last nerve. Hot tears formed at the back of her head as she picked up her phone to call Pam, her bestie.

"Babe, I'm finished this night, please tell me you haven't left the office yet," she cried.

"What has finished you again today? Did that silly landlord show up to harass you again or is it Philip? I have told you that no man has the power to change your smile to a frown, unless he wants me to *change it for him* sharp sharp?" Pamela said.

Buogo replied in a slightly shaky voice, "Babe, please leave Phil out of this, he is innocently sleeping at home. Just leave him be, he'll come around, and somehow I truly believe that this time around it would work out."

Pamela cuts in, "Are you crying? I'm done at the office but the traffic is terrible so I may spend the night here if these trailers don't move before midnight."

"Haaa, babe, it's like your case is worse than my own," she sniffles and dries her eyes.

"So what is it, why are you calling me this night when you're supposed to be soaking in your bathtub with champagne or something light? Or, is today not your day-off?"

"My dear, this kind of day-off where my boss still emailed me a list of new accounts to process, saying, I am the only person she trusts to do a good work. I just finished now and realized it is past 8pm and I didn't make any plans for dinner. And the only thing I want to eat now is that soft milk rolls bread at the mall with that ginger juice from Nelly's."

"Buogo, you and this your midnight bread and juice again? What happened to your diet group and your two weeks of No flour, no sugar and no meat?"

"Haaa, they removed me from the group ooo, I mistakenly posted my dinner of double-portion jollof rice with *Asun* and chilled coke on the group and the admin sent me a message saying I had gone against the group rules by posting their taboo food on a night we were supposed to all eat tofu and bananas. "

"Hahahahaha, banana for dinner, as monkey or what? Babe, wait o, is she the same person that used to send you those silly messages about portion control anytime you post food on your status."

"Yes, the chief monitoring spirit of my nutritional destiny."

They both laugh long and hard and continue in their chit-chat, oblivious of the long night ahead of them as the clouds gather. Buogo never did make it to the bakery in time but the trailers did clear off the road and Pam showed up at her doorstep sometime after 11pm soaking wet from the rain, with bread and yoghurt. Somehow, the world was alright tonight.

****

The importance of eating a healthy meal rich in carbohydrates, proteins, fats, vitamins, minerals, fibre and water daily to help build the body, and protect against diseases has been taught us from the first moments of formal education as well as informal education. We hear statements like, *Let your food be your medicine*, and *You are what you eat*, so I am inclined to believe that the benefits of healthy nutrition is largely acknowledged by most of us. But how many times have we rolled your eyes at the phrase, *You are what you eat*, especially while munching away at a decadent bar of chocolate or your favorite snack. And not because we do not agree with the assertion but because we are simply tired of the many ways society has policed women about what they should and should not eat per time. We just want to eat what we want to eat, when we want to eat it and how we want to eat it, without the food police coming at us and if we're lucky, without getting fat.

Out of respect to all the women who have been food-shamed over the years, let us take a different approach in the discussion of Nutrition as an integral part of holistic living. So let's agree not to dwell only on the benefits of healthy nutrition, which you probably already know anyway, instead, let's just jump right to the heart of the matter. The **How** of Healthy Nutrition.

I know that as women, we have been faced with a barrage of suggestions over issues concerning our weight, cravings during pregnancy and menstruation, diet plans, and even eating disorders. Everybody has an opinion and sometimes neglects to put your peculiar situations like available time, food preferences, food taboos, family size, and resources available, etc into consideration. In looking at nutrition, please free your mind from all judgment and from every limitation that has been placed on you by advertising and the gossip-mill. Let's just be honest and realistic as we explore the basics of healthy eating for busy professionals as well as stay-home and work-from-home wives/mums. As usual, I will talk about what I know and have tested and found to be true. While I am not yet a nutrition expert, I have certainly had my fair share of drama surrounding healthy nutrition, so let's just agree to be as realistic as possible, taking it one small step at a time. No outrageous meal plans and no starving ourselves in the name of portion control. Hopefully, what is working for me may work for you as well.

3.1 CRAVINGS

Your cravings are valid. I feel like I need to get that out of the way before saying anything else. My experience as a restaurateur who caters to women and their families has given me a sense of appreciation, and sometimes wonder, for the patterns of our cravings. I have worked with food for so long that I sometimes imagine I have a sixth sense about food. I love interacting with people, and so for the first few years at my restaurants, I often elected to speak with our clients on phone and take their food orders personally. We developed database of our client's food preferences so that our customer service and satisfaction is better guaranteed. And so, when a woman calls me to order a particular meal, I can somewhat tell what she may be going through and if she is having a really great week or a stressful one. The uncanny one is that I have always been able to guess when a client is pregnant. This information is essential because, at all McOlivia Kitchens, we are careful to advise food choices based on information the client is willing to share. So whenever I discover that a woman is pregnant, there are some food spices that work best in the meals we prepare for her to ensure mother and baby are safe and healthy, while there are some foods and spices that are better left out, depending on the pregnancy stage. I used to think my guesses were just lucky anytime I ask a client if she's pregnant and I get a blushing yes or a, *how did you know*, or an excited, *oh yeah, I just found out this week,* until I realized there's a science behind it.

Because my restaurant's menu is tailored towards cuisine that satisfy nostalgic cravings, it is highly likely that we would get clients who are mostly disposed to cravings, chief of whom are pregnant women. And if you talk with and listen to pregnant women long enough, you tend to know when you hear it in a woman's voice. As a mother, I had my fair share of cravings when I was pregnant, from the whimsical to the downright outrageous like fried rice prepared with just cucumbers. It was hilarious. And I had some strong food aversion too so I didn't even cook for the most part of my pregnancy, I just couldn't stand the smell of food cooking in my kitchen. I hosted a show for over a year on radio concerning Women Health during pregnancy where I got to learn a lot about pregnancy from listening to health experts and pregnant women in that time. It turns out that, as the miracle of a new life is forming inside a woman, her body begins to desire certain foods to prepare itself for the journey of motherhood. Most times, these present as cravings, to push a woman to really get what she needs and help ready her for childbirth, breastfeeding and even the advancing pregnancy. Interestingly, our interpretation of our cravings result in outrageous food demands sometimes. So if the body wants calcium and signals for calcium, we may simply pick up these signals as a craving for shawarma or in the case of most Igbo women nzu (calabash clay). Funny stuff.

I believe that the more trained we are to know what our body really needs in pregnancy and at other times, the more apt we may be in our interpretation of these craving signals. This is why I am in favor of starting ante-natal visits early and asking our care-givers the right questions on pregnancy nutrition, because sometimes they forget to offer this information unless we ask. I suppose that if you let a health professional know what you are craving, they may know what your body really needs and advise same, taking your medical history into consideration.

> **Next time that overwhelming sugar rush hits, perhaps we can take a second to consider what we really need.**

I learned a neat trick from a friend, which is to strategically eliminate foods I like but would prefer not to eat from my immediate environment, and instead to stock up on tasty healthier preferences such that whenever I get a sugar rush or craving, my only available choices are mostly healthy. How can you eat it when you don't have it readily available and within reach?. It seemed like a punishment at first, but with time, it has proven useful and helped me cut down on junks and embrace more healthy food.

So let us consider what we may need to put in place to be sure that we are always able to eat what we honestly desire in a way that nourishes our body.

3.2 HEALTHY NUTRITION

Growing up, we were taught that there are six main classes of food which include carbohydrates, proteins, minerals, vitamins, fats and oil and water. Oh we recited it so passionately in Agric classes that it stuck in my head. When I got old enough to use the internet, I realized some persons also consider fibre as a 7th nutrient necessary for good health. It is ideal to incorporate these food nutrients in the quantity that our body requires, understanding that our individual nutritional needs differ depending on our peculiar circumstances. If one woman is trying to get pregnant, and another woman is trying to manage diabetes or add weight, they need different things. Therefore healthy nutrition for each woman would depend largely on her own needs. You can work with a nutritionist to determine your own nutritional needs if you feel unsure about them.

3.3 MEAL PLANNING

Why Choose a Meal Plan?

After we have decided what our peculiar nutritional needs may be, then a meal plan is the next best strategy to help us stay on our chosen path. Having a meal plan means we get to consciously prioritize those nutrients our body needs, and match it as closely as possible to the foods that we enjoy eating, occasionally tweaking portions and enjoying varieties within those identified food options. There are some foods that nobody can ever force us to eat no matter how nutritious they say it is. Creating our own meal plan is just a way we get to stay on top of our nutritional game without anybody compelling us to do what we don't want. Of course, meal planning is not magic. So, a little patience can go a long way to ensure we don't get frustrated with the entire process.

Components of an Ideal Meal Plan

In order for our meal plan to succeed and be sustainable, there are a few things to consider, including;

- **Specificity and Desirabilify:** Try to personalize your meal plan to include foods that you love to eat, and not foods that you are allergic to or that you consider as food taboos. If you don't eat snails, do not include it in your meal plan. If you are allergic to honey, then don't have it in your meal plan. If you are vegan, pescetarian, vegetarian etc, then it is only natural that it is reflected in your meal plan. Do your best to incorporate your favorite foodstuff into your menu plan for versatility and *enjoyability*. For instance, my husband and daughter love beans and all bean-based foods so each week, our menu tries to feature at least one variant of a beans meal like porridge beans with potato/plantains, or moi-moi (beans pudding), or akara (bean fritters) etc. I love fruits and vegetables so we also try to have one type of vegetable soup,, fruit salads and smoothies weekly. Meal time can be as fun as possible when we incorporate what we love. But occasionally we would miss out on these meals and that is just okay because nobody is coming to our house to inspect or monitor what we eat. You can try listing the foods you love and noting how many variations you can make from each particular meal. It may seem like a silly exercise but you may be surprised what you find out when you deliberately think about what you like eating and write it out, Take potatoes for example, we can boil, fry , roast, grill, and even bake potatoes and enjoy them. It is okay to experiment with food if that's your thing but it is also okay to stick with what you know. The important thing is to look out for food sources that provide what you need, whether you're a student, a bosslady, a mother or even a pregnant woman etc. Eat what you love, and know that your nutrition is your responsibility.

- **Ease of preparation:** I wish there was a way to cook some of our favorite meals in just five minutes. Or even a way to just click on a link on the internet and download food immediately when we are hungry and tired. I mean, that would be a big hit for most of us. But alas, technology has refused to advance in that direction yet. So while the experts are still working on that, we may just need to concentrate on meals that we can easily prepare. As fun as it can be to try new recipes, we can try to just reduce our frustration with meal planning by starting off casually with meals that we find easy to prepare. Some meals require longer hours to prepare, so it may be best to leave such meals for days when there is less work or more hands to help. Fried rice can take longer to prepare than porridge potatoes, for instance. And potatoes can take more time to prepare than oats. So an ideal meal plan should simply take available time into consideration. Meal Planning becomes sustainable when we incorporate foods that we enjoy but that don't take the entire day, leaving little time for much else. This is probably why nuts, teas, oats, fruits, and vegetables are a great hit for breakfast because they require very little time to prepare as they are mostly enjoyed raw or without much cooking. Imagine having to prepare Jollof Rice for breakfast when you have to be at work by 7am. While it may be possible for some time, it may get tiring eventually.

- **Affordability and Ease of Access:** more often than not, foodstuff that are locally grown, are fresher and more accessible ,especially when they are in season. And for some food produce, they can be more affordable too. For instance, corn is fresher, more accessible, and affordable, and are more likely to contain little or no preservatives during the rainy season. I find that generally, the farther a food produce is imported, the higher the chance of chemical preservatives, which are harmful to health. So it serves to keep this is mind when meal planning and go for foods that are in season.

- Variety and Flexibility: the less strict our meal plan, the more likely that we will commit to it. I don't know why this happens but I just know that human beings don't enjoy the feeling of being boxed in. So, it may help if we leave a little room for surprises. It is okay to drink garri with groundnut and milk on an afternoon where our menu says we should be eating spaghetti and meatballs. No need to feel guilty, as long as we can get back to the meal plan when we are ready. And of course, variety is still considered the spice of life by most. So let's switch things up occasionally by ordering out or dining out when we feel the need.

3.4 BASIC GARDENING TIPS

The primary role of nutrition is nourishment for the body and nature has an abundance of food items to fulfill that role. However, as the rise in foodstuff prices get more and more outrageous even in the local markets, nature might just be calling us back to gardening or subsistence farming. To reduce the family cost on feeding, vegetables, herbs and spices can be planted in small pots and give an appreciable amount of harvest that ensures the family nutritional needs are met at lower costs. Gardening can also be a therapeutic hobby and some gardeners I know say it can help one grow the virtue of patience, tenderness and love. Growing up, my parents who had white-collar jobs always tended small farms that provided us our basic yam, cassava, pineapples, pawpaw, vegetables and sometimes during the rainy season, my mum's farm yielded lots of crabs. They were such a yummy delicacy in soups, even though I haven't eaten them in a while.

My friend Onyinye, has over two hundred varieties of plants in her home garden. She also has some really cute animals there like white rabbits and turtles. With time, she has built Savvy Gardens to become a business that helps others start and grow their own gardens. In my recent interview with her, Onyi shared these few tips that any woman who wishes to start her own garden will find useful.

❖ Start Small. Whether you are gardening as a hobby or for food or both, feel free to begin with just a few seeds per time. The less you over think it, the more likely you are to start already.

❖ Plant what you and your family will enjoy eating. If Okra soup is your favorite, then plant Okra. If tomatoes make a repeated appearance in your weekly grocery list, consider planting tomatoes.

❖ Plant according to the season and your clime. Find plants that do well in your region and consider the best season for planting same.

❖ Know the plants you are growing. This implies that you need to know as much as possible about the plant. What type of soil is best for the plant, what about mulching? what amount of water and sunlight does it require, what insects are likely to attack it and how do you defend it, does your plant need any physical support or does your plant have any special nutritional requirements and how long does it take before you can expect a harvest? These information keep you honest in your expectations and realistic about the adventure you're embarking on.

❖ Give it time. Patience is one of the things that gardening will teach you. Be patient and wait for a bountiful harvest. Even if it is just a handful of *habanero* peppers, one harvest will often lead to many more.

One more thing to consider in gardening is the refreshing and clean air that comes with it. It can do wonders for our mental and emotional health, as well, Onyinye says.

As Ken Druse puts it, 'When gardeners garden, it is not just plants that grow but gardeners themselves'.

3.5 MEAL PREP

Meal prepping is an important aspect of meal planning which involves readying parts of the intended cooking ahead of time. This can be a time-saver as it reduces the time spent when cooking the meals. For example, we can blend the crayfish for the incoming week's cooking over the weekend and put oats for the week into smaller containers and store in a small pantry.

I prefer to lay out all the ingredients required for each meal on a tray, as well as the appropriate pots and pans tray, as it helps with clarity and reduces time spent once cooking starts. It also makes it easier for me to sit down in breaks during cooking and delegate other kitchen roles to any other person available to help. I find that identifying the ingredients in their right amounts, as well as the cooking utensils etc that are necessary for preparing a particular meal makes it easier to delegate recipes to kitchen assistants and any other person available to help, in a way that makes it easier to reproduce the taste and consistency of the meal. So perhaps this is one way we can maximize our time in the kitchen without having to live in the kitchen as some suggest we should.

We can conveniently meal prep for a variety of meals and store them in the fridge or pantry, in a way that we can have the ingredients half-ready when we are ready to cook, for example, pepper sauce, jam, blended herbs and spices for marinating fish and meat, as well as diced carrots and other veggies, being careful to use them within a few days for maximum taste and health benefits. Since meal prepping requires us to determine and somewhat prepare for what to eat ahead of time, it may help us stay committed to our nutritious food choices. Sometimes one can be just so tired but then you remember that you have meal prepped and it will only take a few minutes to make a particular meal on your menu, and it just gives you the energy to even try.

3.6 SDG GOAL 2: ZERO HUNGER

In order to achieve Goal 2 of the Sustainable Development Goals, which seeks to end hunger, achieve food security and improved nutrition and promote sustainable agriculture, I believe that Personal and Family Nutrition is paramount. Through my non-governmental organization, McOlivia Foundation, I have organized food drives and donations to the indigent in our society and fed several poor and vulnerable children. While that is a good move, I think an even better and more sustainable move would be for those of us who have the means to healthy nutrition, to take personal responsibility for our personal and family nutrition by incorporating nourishing and delicious meal options into our menu and lifestyle. Maybe then, the United Nations will declare all of us global ambassadors for the SDG Goal 2: Zero Hunger. Of course I'm joking, but it wouldn't hurt if somehow we find a way to eat healthy and stay happy. It's the least we can do for ourselves for the awesome work we do every day. Just imagine being a certified *foodie* with a medal of honor simply for eating right.

Simple Menu Ideas

Breakfast

Breakfast is often referred to as the most important meal of the day. For this reason, something light and easy to prepare may be a good choice to get us ready for the day ahead. Here are some meal choices to consider for breakfast, depending on our nutritional needs, and other factors we looked at earlier.

- Cakes, muffins, doughnuts etc

- Sausages

- Puddings e.g Moi-moi (bean pudding), okpa (bambara puddinng)

- Cereals

- Sandwiches

- Akara (bean fritters)

- Oats

- Smoothies

- Pancakes and waffles

- Fruit Salads

- Vegetable Salads

- Mixed Salads that incorporate meat, poultry or seafood.

- Non-alcoholic Beverages e.g cocoa, tea, coffee, milk, fruit juice, yoghurt etc.

- Eggs (poached, fried or scrambled).

- Mushrooms.

- Bread and Toast with Preserves/butter.

Brunch

Brunch may seem like something for *bougiee* girls, the way they say it in movies, but far from it. Interestingly, the word Brunch is a portmanteau of breakfast and lunch. So, If we miss breakfast, then brunch to the rescue. If we don't have plans for lunch, then brunch to the rescue.

Some simple ideas for Brunch;

- ➤ Nuts e.g Groundnuts, Almonds, Pistachios, Cashew nuts , Walnuts, Hazelnuts.

- ➤ Beverages e.g herbal teas, juice, coffee, champagne etc.

- ➤ Croissant, crepe, waffles, cinnamon rolls, biscuits etc.

- ➤ Fruits e.g Apples, Oranges, watermelon, pineapples, avocados etc.

- ➤ Egg dishes e.g Eggs Benedict, Fried egg, Omelette, Poached egg, Scrambled eggs etc.

Lunch & Dinner

I recently discovered that lunch used to be reserved for ladies only, up until the early 19th century. Imagine a world where only women ate lunch. What would we even do with all the hungry men on our hands? I think it's a good thing that everyone is allowed to eat lunch in the 21st century.

Consider some of these meal ideas for lunch or dinner. As a celebration of my cultural identity, I have deliberately highlighted some traditional Nigerian cuisine here. It may be great to try some out if you love experimenting with new food. I believe there are recipes online.

Nigerian Staples

*For maximum satisfaction, we enjoy these staples as pottage, or boiled/roasted/baked/fried/broiled, etc and pair with one or more thick or thin soups, stews or sauces.

YAM, POTATOES, PLANTAINS, COCOYAM, BEANS, CORN, RICE.

Other popular staples; PUDDINGS LIKE MOI-MOI, OKPA, Tuwo, ekpang nkukwo.

SWALLOW like Eba, Fufu, Pounded Yam, Wheat, Elubo, Amala, etc,

Abacha, Ugba , Gizdodo, Agidi/eko, Ewa Aganyin, Nkwobi, Isiewu.

Thin Soups; Beef & Plantain Peppersoup, Goatmeat Peppersoup, Chicken Peppersoup, Turkey, Peppersoup, Fresh Fish Peppersoup, Liver Soup, Nsala Soup.

Vegan Thin Soups; Onion Soup, Mushroom soup, Yam Peppersoup, Plantain Peppersoup.

Thick Soups; Gbegiri soup, Oha soup, Banga soup, Ewedu Soup, Groundnut soup, Egusi Soup, Ogbono Soup, Bitterleaf soup.

Vegetable Soups; Okra Soup, Efo Riro Soup, Edika-ikong Soup, Afang Soup, Atama Soup.

Nigerian Sauces and Stews; Vegetable stew, Fresh tomato stew, Carrot stew, Egusi stew, Fish sauce, Egg sauce, Ugba sauce, Kpomo sauce, Onion sauce, Liver sauce, Beef/Chicken curry sauce, Snail sauce, Vegetable stir fry.

Nigerian Rice Meals; Fried Rice, Coconut Rice, Vegetable Rice, Palm Oil Jollof Rice, Nigerian Jollof Rice, Jollof Rice and Beans, Rice and stew/sauce.

Sample Meal Timetable

Having a meal timetable would save us the time and energy spent on a daily basis trying to figure out what to eat. This sample is simply a guide for you to draw up your own using the information shared earlier on in this chapter. Feel free to add what works for you as Breakfast, Lunch and Dinner, in your own meal time table from Monday to Sunday. The brunch option is just there for days you miss breakfast or have no plans for lunch.

Breakfast	Brunch	Lunch	Dinner
Oats with Milk and sugar paired with egg and apple.	Carrot Cake and Orange juice.	Potato and Tomato Stew	Fish Peppersoup and Coleslaw

Generic Meal Timetable

Breakfast	Brunch	Lunch	Dinner
Pick a meal from your list of breakfast ideas.	Select from your list of brunch ideas.	Select from your list of lunch ideas.	Select from your list of dinner ideas.

3.7 BASIC DINING ETIQUETTE

If we can find a way to keep our phones on silent or our eyes off the T.V during meal time, in order to respect the sanctity of the meal, enjoy the social presence of fellow diners and practise mindfulness, then I think we will be just fine.

Being mindful suggests that we pay attention as we savor our meal instead of just munching away mindlessly. I think this is one of the most important dining etiquettes we need to add to all the other ones we learnt growing up. Whether alone or in company of others, experts suggest that practicing mindfulness may help us curb overeating.

3.8 MEAL HACKS FOR WEIGHT LOSS

What if one day we learn that there is really no shortcut to weight loss? That would be such heartbreaking news, especially for those who spend much of their earnings on slimming teas with all promises of weight loss. I cannot say if slimming teas work or not, but I do think that some amount of work and diligence is necessary for any true lasting change to occur. In Chapter 4, we will look at the Body Mass Index, which can be a great tool to calculate and determine what normal weight range for each individual is. If we find out that we are underweight or overweight, then proper nutrition and dieting may play a big role in addressing it. Exercise can also help. One can speak to a nutritionist or health professional to determine a meal plan that can help her stay healthy within the desired weight range.

Here are a few steps that helped me lose weight after weaning my daughter off breast milk. Some of them are things I learned from my 3 year course in Food and Nutrition while in college, while others were recommended by a nutritionist. This was designed with me in mind, so it may not be a perfect fit for you. I hope that it can help you design your own process taking into consideration, your age, nutritional needs, preferences, available funds, lifestyle, family size and your nutritional goal etc;

My Age: 30.

Preferences: Local and African cuisine.

Nutritional Goal: Post-Partum weight loss and General Health.

Lifestyle: Sedentary worker with an occasional need for energy burst to chase my daughter around or host an event.

Some of the dietary adjustments to achieve my desired goal included the following;

Reduced consumption of processed foods like noodles and pasta, as well as heavily preserved foods, bread and processed flour. I will eat these if they are the only option but try not to make them a constant feature.

Incorporated thin soups like nsala, peppersoup, liver soup etc and vegetable soups like afang, edika-ikong etc into my menu, while reducing thick soups like egusi, and palm oil soup (ofeakwu).

Snack on, mostly fruits, vegetables and nuts like peanuts, cashew nuts, cucumber, carrots, etc, instead of junks.

Reduced consumption of foods fried in oil and opted for healthier cooking options like boiling, simmering, broiling, grilling and baking.

Reduced consumption of rice, that is, until my husband prepares Nigerian Jollof and I lose focus temporarily.

Reduced consumption of drinks with artificial sweeteners like soft drinks and chose healthier alternatives like fruit smoothies, Zobo drink, Fruit juice, and occasionally yoghurt. As well as healthy teas like Hibiscus tea (Zobo), ginger tea, Cocoa tea with milk etc.

Increased consumption of green leafy vegetables and made my own salad dressing which can be a healthier and more affordable option.

Replaced artificial flavors with organic condiments like *ogili*, thyme, nutmeg, crayfish, garlic, ginger, bayleaf, basil, curry etc.

Last but certainly not least, I stopped skipping meals and started to pay more attention to my food when eating.

There is no pressure, and as long as we acknowledge that good nutrition is a journey and not a destination, then we will be patient with our personal journey. I did not lose all the weight brought on by motherhood overnight, but at least I am neither underweight nor overweight at the moment, and that is good enough for me. Once in a while I check my weight and I am happy with my slow but steady progress. I recently found out that I fit into my old shorts again and that felt fantastic. Everything else will come with time, if we do not lose faith in our process.

> **In designing a meal plan or diet plan, I suppose small changes sustained over a long period of time are better than big and dramatic changes that we may soon get tired of. Let's go easy on ourselves.**

3.9 FOOD PLAITING

Food plating is the art of arranging food in a way that makes it aesthetically pleasing to the eye. This can help boost our appetite and a well plaited meal sends the signal that we matter and you are worth the effort of a well presented meal. As a restaurateur, excellent food presentation has always been one of my game changers at McOlivia's Kitchen and one of the major differences between my meals and its *cheaper* competition. One day, it occurred to me that if I put the same efforts I put into serving clients an appetizing meal into my own home kitchen, the result would be fantastic. So I set out to slowly and strategically replace all my dinnerware (crockery) and cutlery and add a dash of creativity into some of my bowls and plates, the result is a kitchen that looks satisfying to the eyes and meals that not only taste delicious but look irresistible.

I know food plaiting may sound like something for restaurants and food vendors, but you can try it at home. Cook yourself a nice meal, serve in a beautiful white dish with gold cutlery, and take your time to be creative with the food design on the plate (Pinterest has beautiful food plaiting options and YouTube can show you videos). If you don't have gold and white sets, use what you have available and I bet that you would feel like a true queen when you serve yourself this meal knowing how much love and deliberate thought was put into it.

What a refreshing confidence boost it brings to be served like royalty. I am raising my daughter to only accept the best treatment and to walk away from shabby treatments in life, and it begins with how her food is presented at home. She is always eager to finish her meals because they always look so good. Even my husband knows that, irrespective of what meal is being served, there is a standard of beauty and burst of colors that come with every meal. You can practically taste the love in every bite. With time, I have trained my kitchen assistants and chefs both at my restaurants and at home to embody that same meticulous and refreshing service that transforms a simple meal to a million dollar cuisine and makes meal time something to look forward to everyday. I didn't always used to know this but over time I have learnt to be deliberate with my meals and it makes such a great difference. So perhaps you may want to try it and see how it works for you. Do it for yourself, do it for your family. Do it for a day, and if you like the results, do it for a week, and then a month, till it becomes a part of your lifestyle. If you feel like you failed at first attempt, congratulate yourself for even trying and try again till it works. You deserve only the finest things in life. Money cannot buy this special treatment, it comes from a place of genuine appreciation of self and an understanding that we truly deserve the best as the Queens we are!

Now that we have explored the woman and her nutrition, whether she is single or in a relationship, a business woman or career woman, a wife or a mother, who is fueled not just by passion but by a belly full of yummy nutritious food, I believe she has the full strength to advance on this journey of holistic living. In the next chapter, we look at the woman at Work, an absolute Boss Lady.

One Cannot Think well, love well,
sleep well, if one has not dined well.
-Virginia Woolf.

CHAPTER 4
WORK

Buogo had a hunch that the lady that just moved next door was a big time executive.

First, because she had taken the only fully furnished building in the estate and secondly, she seemed to always have time to work out. It had been two months now since she came into the estate but it was only this morning that she found out her name. Adjoa, she had replied when Buogo asked, in what seemed the softest voice for a woman of her build. She was often up and running whenever Buogo was leaving for work. And not figuratively. She was dressed in the finest joggers that seemed to hug her plump figure pretty well every morning and always looked ready to run a mile in a minute.

In the two times they had exchanged pleasantries, she could never quite hold Adjoa's attention because her gaze was always shifting as she looked ahead. Today was no different but somehow she had managed to get a name, and that was some good progress. For some reasons she could not explain, she knew that Adjoa would fit right into her circle. She seemed nice enough, and young enough, although she couldn't tell if she was single or married. It wouldn't matter anyway.

She hadn't seen her with any family but by the sound of her name and accent, Buogo had immediately suspected she wasn't from around the country. Adjoa was definitely not a Nigerian name. She was almost at the office now, perhaps Lara or Chrissy, two of her favorite colleagues, would know the name. And guess who would greet her as she stepped out of the elevator onto her office floor?

Lara the Great. Everybody loved Lara. Maybe because she was resourceful or because she seemed like she had a firm grasp of her own worth as a woman. Whatever the reason, Lara was the girl everybody wanted to have on the team when there was a deadline. She knew how to rally everyone around and exuded such confidence that made her leadership easy to follow. She was not a manager yet, but on three occasions, she had been named the Employee of the Month, even though Buogo could swear that she was way more committed to the job and more qualified. But she was never envious of Lara. It was difficult to envy Lara whose story everybody knew. She had lost her parents in a car accident and grew up in an orphanage and somehow managed to train herself in school with the occasional support of the orphanage home. Yet, nobody knew why she remained single till date. She was gracious, beautiful, smart and at 38, had successfully built an impeccable reputation that made most clients request her as their account manager. She never pretended to be perfect but two cosmetic surgeries later, it was clear to everyone that she was dedicated to maintaining a specific body image at all costs. And oh, she reveled in her beauty and was upfront about the cost of her plastic surgery whenever anybody asked. Lara, the Great, was everybody's go-to girl but nobody's plaything.

So, when Buogo flashed a smile at Lara and instead of the usual hug, Lara raised her left hand to show off the most exquisite engagement ring, it took a moment for Buogo to close her mouth and collect her thoughts. All questions about the investigation into the name Adjoa flew out the window together with her sense of decorum. She let out an excited screech and jumped straight into Lara's open arms. She caught a tear as they hugged tightly in a memorable embrace. Lara was the only other single lady in her department and now she was all alone. Yet, joy welled up inside her as she disengaged from the warm hug and exclaimed. "Congratulations, my darling. Now come and tell me how you went from *single pringle* to engaged in the blink of an eye. Who is this very lucky, mystery man, who has swept our Lara off her feet so?"

****

In this chapter, we look at the many faces a woman can wear at work, as we discuss work in the context of how every woman can succeed in her workplace, daily and in the long run. A woman may choose to volunteer at a job for several reasons, or she can run a business, work in a charity organization, be an employer or employee, enjoy the thrill of being an entrepreneur or intraprenuer, or be the ultimate home manager. Whether paid or unpaid service, part-time or full-time, it is important for every woman to have a work they can do to fulfill that need in us to apply ourselves and be relevant. Solving a need and being part of the solution in our society is a vital aspect for holistic living, not only for men but for women, as well.

A woman can work in one or more of the following and so we will explore her opportunities along these 3 basic work lines;

1. The Career Woman.

2. The Entrepreneur Woman.

3. The Home Manager Woman.

4.1 THE CAREER WOMAN

I got a long message one morning from someone who would like me to mentor them on the path of event hosting, praising my works and highlighting some of my accomplishments and the message took me down a long memory lane.

One of the first things to build in oneself if you must succeed is, Believe in Self. It is non-negotiable, and if we don't have self confidence, people may crush us at every turn and may often take advantage of us. When I started out in my Media Career, I was a young impressionable On Air Personality working as a Radio and TV Presenter, with a lot of talent but not much training yet. For what it was worth, I was quite popular and well loved even at that stage. I naturally got the opportunity to interview some top celebrities in the music and movie industry on my Radio and TV shows, but I wasn't nearly as self confident then as I am today.

So one day, a popular movie actor, Genevieve Nnaji was coming to our radio station for an interview and I was asked to host the interview. But only because my colleague was unavailable that day, they said. So I declined the offer to interview her because I wasn't willing to open myself up to any criticism and I definitely wasn't willing to hear I didn't do well enough after the interview.

I had a colleague who made it his mission to convince me that I wasn't good enough and who insisted that I was a rookie even over a year after we started working together. And this greatly chipped at my self confidence. While it was understandable that his constant negativity had this effect on me, the truth remains that the responsibility for my growth and success lies entirely on my shoulders. Granted, it is great when people believe in us and encourage us but even when they don't, for reasons we cannot help, we must always believe in ourself.

I also had a colleague who called me aside that day and tried to encourage me and reassure me that the interview was not a big deal, and that I was truly good enough. Still, the voice of self-doubt in my head was louder than his voice, I guess.

The funny thing is, I'm not sure she came to the station again for that interview but I'm pretty sure I didn't interview her that day. I had robbed myself of the opportunity to advance in my career simply because I chose to align my assessment of my abilities with a false negative report rather than a true positive report. This was tantamount to self-sabotage, but it was the last I ever sabotaged myself and career in that way.

I wrote that to say these;

✧   Stop depending on the validation of other people.

✧   Start validating yourself by yourself.

Navigating Workplace Politics

As women, we must not continue to be intimidated by the unseen glass ceiling rumored to limit women in the work place. If we will rise to the peak of our potentials, and not be limited by workplace politics, we have to be deliberate about equipping ourselves to become masters of the game. As a woman, I believe that some of the best strategies to equip oneself to excel in workplace politics and advance in your career are;

1) Build Competence: Put in the work and actually learn your job. I found that the more training and research I did, the less inadequate I felt and the better I got at my job. People will still try to put you down for many different reasons, sometimes deliberately and sometimes they're just being ignorant or they have unresolved issues in their own lives. But you have to learn to remove your focus from these other people. Let them argue about your methods but let your results speak for you always. It cost me some money and time to attend workshops and develop myself but they were absolutely worth it. I began to get nominations in several categories for my work as a Radio and TV presenter at this time and by 2017, I was recognized by the Enugu State Government as one of 50 most Influential youth in the state, appointed to mentor other young persons. This recognition came as a result of the impact of my NGO, McOlivia's Foundation, and my work in using the media as a tool for positive change in the society.

Two years after the interview incident mentioned above, I was invited to come on set for Genevieve Nnaji's Lionheart. Someone in her crew reached out personally to me to audition for the role of the TV Presenter. I did and I got the role. Then I got to meet Genevieve, and other cast and crew on set. For some reason, production of the movie was halted for some months. When the production resumed a few months later and I was called to set again, I declined because my priorities had changed and I had moved on to other things, away from the Coal City where the film was shot. A decision I do not regret. I am happy at the success and wide acceptance of the movie after it's adoption by Netflix. And even happier to have developed myself into a woman with priorities and enough options to turn such an offer down gracefully. When we build competence in ourselves as women, it comes with such an empowering force of confidence, that we begin to effortlessly prioritize and choose only what serves our best interests in our career growth. This is how we present ourselves with options and can safely walk away from what doesn't serve us and only into what allows us to be our best selves.

2) Update your CV: as you grow, never lose sight of the things you've learned and accomplished and always document these learning, accomplishments and improvements. Your experiences and accomplishments qualify you, and are the best bargaining tools for better opportunities and better work remuneration. As a media personality, I learned to put videos together, beyond just profiles and CVs, and use same as part of my project bids, and these have opened doors to big projects in the 12 years that I have hosted events across several industries.

I've gone on to interview notable personalities on radio, TV, and on live red carpets, including Bank executives, founders, superstar entertainers, political and religious leaders.

In one event production incident, I was scheduled to interview some celebrites for Africa Magic. It was way past midnight and my producer had released me to go to my hotel, even though we had not yet interviewed some of the VVIP celebrities that would make the headlines. So, although I had the option to leave, I had grown to become quite committed to the demands of my job so I waited anyway, outside in the cold around 1am instead of sitting in the cozy lounge reserved for us, because I knew that staying outdoors improved my chances of getting these interviews for my team. I had become the person that takes charge of my life and every responsibility placed in my hands. I no longer had excuses and no longer waited for any validation. I showed up whenever I was needed and I delivered every job as excellently as I could. And my new found confidence came from a place of self development and an acknowledgement of my God-given abilities.

I attached photos of my interview with Chimamanda Adichie, Davido, Professor Lumumba and others here for several reasons especially so that if you're at a place in your life where you feel like the old me that I described up there; impressionable, insecure, naive, and an absolute rookie, you would know that it is possible to rise above all that uncertain beginning and truly excel at the things that used to scare you.

I reflected these experiences and improvements in my CVs and profiles. I made sure everyone knew it, my name is McOlivia, I am an exceptional event MC and I go the extra mile to deliver value and excellence. It wasn't long before I went from being undervalued to commanding the deserved respect and getting the honor of traveling with a fully sponsored team for my events. Even as a mum, I have had several brands provide flight, and all necessary logistics to ensure that I travel with my daughter and her care-giver to host their events. This for me, is living life on my own terms, experiencing the best of both worlds, being a mother who is always present in the life of the child she loves, whilst continuing to grow in a career she adores.

And because I could do it, I am inclined to believe that we all can We can develop ourselves and whe we do, we must shout it from the rooftops, never being afraid to demand what we're worth at every time. We can have it all, even as women. We can have the best of both worlds.

3) Build Strategic Relationships: Workplace politics doesn't seem to be going away anytime soon, so to ensure we continue to grow in our career, let us endeavour to sharpen our human relationship skills. I am not advocating that one becomes a doormat or answers Yes to every person's demands just to be likeable, but rather that we be strategic in our Yes and No. Know what your deliverables are, and while you work on them, be nice to your colleagues and superiors or subordinates. There are doors that may remain closed to us until we learn how to be a team player. This is the one thing I learned later on in my career that opened more doors than my talents and skills combined ever could. It is simply being good at people management, and this not only makes our work and life easier, but may be the key to rising to a position of leadership or getting a raise or promotion. Interestingly, that particular colleague of mine who used to undermine my efforts at work has become an ally today, and while we are honest about our earlier work disagreements, it doesn't deny us of any future business, marked with mutual respect. I have access to his network and his experience, because I worked on myself, became confident and stopped seeing him as an irritable liability but managed him like an asset.

As we go along in life, we grow, and so we must outgrow any patterns and behaviors that don't serve us. If you find out that you are always unlucky in your work place, find out what the challenge may be. Sometimes a little adjustment in your personal work ethics and service delivery goes a long way. But other times you just need to get the right person in your corner, rooting for you in private meetings where promotions and opportunities are discussed. This is one of the reasons why some people keep advancing in their career even when it seems they do not qualify for it. Human relationships play a major role in career advancement.

4) Become a Team Player: At YALI, the fellowship for Young African leaders, instituted by President Barack Obama, I was selected for several roles that were media-related but bordered more on my human relationship skills, evidenced by my emotional quotient (EQ) rather than my Intelligence Quotient (IQ). I suspect so, because there were a few tasks that I did not judge myself the most qualified but that were handed to me amidst over a hundred African leaders from different countries. For instance, I was once given a sensitive task to complete in a very short time. At the time of the fellowship, I was the General Manager of a radio station back in Nigeria, and so it may have been easy for the organizers and facilitators to consider me capable. But deep in my heart, I knew this was not a task I could deliver excellently and in time, unless I worked with a team. I am realistic about my strengths, and I'm never too proud to admit my limitations, and this has proven one of my strongest capabilities. So I worked on identifying some other young leaders who would make great team players and help me deliver on the project. I spoke to our program administrator who had assigned me this task at this time and explained how time may present a difficulty in delivering the quality of work assigned and I went a step further to submit the names of those I had identified as qualified to join me in the work. She was visibly and audibly impressed by my identification of the problem, and the solutions I had proffered. So, yes, she did let me put a team together and supervise the team, and yes, we did deliver before the deadline she had initially given. So, what may have been impossible for one person to accomplish was excellently delivered by a Team, and everyone was happy, acknowledged and satisfied. A few months later, after the fellowship had ended and we had all gone back to our respective countries, this program administrator reached out to me to become the Country Director for her multinational Business and Investment company, and we have gone ahead to do even bigger projects together in my new role. And we continue to maximize teams in our work together.

Becoming an efficient team player requires a few things, including but not limited to;

➢ An understanding of one's strengths and limitations.

➢ An interest in getting the job done.

➢ A willingness to share the spotlight, including sharing the dividends of success.

➢ A confidence in your abilities.

➢ A willingness to communicate and work with others.

You are not indispensable and the risk most persons quote for not working well in teams is that someone may rise up and take the credit for all their work, so they hold back and are wary of team playing and sharing knowledge in the workplace. My response in recent times has been to document as much as possible, and be professional in my workplace relationships. Copy whoever is worthy of being copied in all official emails. Yes, there may be wolves in sheep clothing waiting to push you under the bus at the slightest opportunity but the onus is on you to stay alert and keep developing yourself thereby making yourself more difficult to get rid of. Be so good at what you do, that even if you ever leave your job, there's always documented proof of what you've done and you can replicate it in other places. Stop letting people force you into playing small, rise and shine. Dare to be a team player, and be the best at it.

5) Mentor and Train Others: Beyond being a team player, one of the most satisfying and yet most frightening place in a woman's career is the place of mentorship. When we get to the place of mentorship, we are ready to empower the next generation after us. This is a frightening place if we are afraid of being displaced or replaced by a younger, possibly more vibrant version of us. As women, our fear sometimes is that if we mentor or train other women in the workplace, we may become redundant or shoot ourselves in the leg. While I admit that this does happen, I think that it may also be a flawed way of looking at it. Personally, I have trained a male subordinate, only for this young man to turn around and try to take over my position. This is selfish and we see it play out every day in the workplace. As painful as this can be, it should not douse our interest in training and empowering others in the workplace. Instead, we can seek to find ways to ensure that as we teach others what we know per time, we do not sabotage ourselves in the process but instead continued to grow and stay relevant. Once we shift our mindset to take personal responsibility, we put a bit more demand on ourselves to pursue personal development such that as we teach what we know, we still continue to learn more and grow exponentially. The satisfying part of mentorship can be the fulfillment that comes from being a part of another woman's success story, and helping others avoid the pitfalls we faced and maximize the processes that worked for us. As a mentor, you are a bridge, making the journey shorter and less lonely for the woman behind you, sharing with them the secrets you wish someone had shown you. While it may seem, at the onset, that we live in a society that doesn't reward mentorship, we would be pleasantly surprised to find that the rewards of mentorship are massive, if we do not give up in your job of mentoring others. One of the greatest rewards is that as we mentor others, we replicate ourselves and become a formidable force in that industry. Awards and recognition go to women such as these. Another interesting reward is the ability to have access to groups and communities that we can recommend for group projects, imagine having 10 women who can do what we do presently and putting them together in a team, the impact would be explosive! We get to finally take a break when we need to, and perhaps go on a vacation, knowing fully well that our protégé is going to handle the job excellently. And last but certainly not least, the more we train and empower others, the more we become an authority in that field. We may never become a legend in an industry if we do not take time to train others.

In 2020, after 11 years of hosting events locally and internationally, as well as producing and presenting several radio and TV shows, interviewing and moderating panel discussions amongst several key industry players, I was able to set up and run The Hosting Academy by McOlivia, which provides training and mentorship for persons in Radio, TV, Public Speakers and Event Hosts etc. Against all odds and amidst the Covid pandemic, the very first edition of this lifetime project was launched with facilitators in the Media, Wellness and Fashion Industry from the UK, USA, and Nigeria. The peculiarities of the Covid pandemic necessitated that the academy was hosted online with participants from Canada, UK, Nigeria etc. Even after only one edition, I am satisfied to ponder on the endless possibilities and opportunities for the participants of the maiden edition and look forward to subsequent editions. The goal, for me, is to die empty, having successfully poured myself out into the women around me. I do not believe that we need to wait till we are perfect before we can mentor another person. Whatever little we know, it is okay to teach someone else. Every opportunity to achieve this goal, including mentorship and authoring this book, I embrace with both hands.

4.2 THE ENTREPRENEUR WOMAN

The Entrepreneur woman initiates, organizes and operates a business concern. Women entrepreneurs are those women who think of a business enterprise, initiate it, organize and combine factors of production, operate the enterprise and undertake risks and handle economic uncertainties involved in running it. This definition is according to Article Library, and I agree with it. May I also add, that a woman entrepreneur is concerned with financial empowerment for herself and in most cases; she is also interested in being an employer of labor now or in the long run.

I am always excited when I meet a woman who has chosen the unpredictable path of entrepreneurship, I think of such a woman as a daring and courageous being, first before everything. To be an entrepreneur is to be a creator, making something out of nothing, and never giving up. So, it is quite a beauty to see women take on such tasks and I am deliberate to celebrate such women everyday and wherever I find them. In Lagos Nigeria, our markets are filled with women who are entrepreneurs and while some are scaling everyday and relocating their business from the markets to more posh locations and branches, others are content to stay within those markets and milk their brand loyalty rooted deeply in predictability.

For years, I have run several businesses successfully so I am what many may refer to as a serial entrepreneur or as I recently learned, a multipreneur. I have done several business courses and have a degree in Economics, evident of my love for business. One particular course may have been the highlight of my academics and may have set me on a sure path to entrepreneurship, even as a teenager. The course was by CEDR, Centre for Entrepreneurship, Development and Research and was arguably the most practical course we took in the university, I suspect it had such a profound impact because of my inherent passion and interests. Right from the University of Nigeria, where I turned my corner of my dorm into a mini-restaurant, preparing different delicacies and employing other students to help in the cooking and distribution process, a love and interest in entrepreneurship blossomed in me. The profits I made went into different things and as is true of most entrepreneurs, part of it went into learning other skills like bag-making, shoe-making, bead making etc, all of which turned to money making ventures on different scales at different times.

When everybody else is in doubt, and is asking why, the entrepreneur has a still, yet commanding voice that asks,

Why not? There is nobody quite as determined as the woman who is willing to try. She will find a way; even where everybody else has declared there is no way, especially if she has a family to feed or is widowed or a single mother.

What Works For Women in Entrepreneurship

There are 3 C's which I believe are a game changer for every woman in business, irrespective of the industry she finds herself in, they include;

COMPETENCE

One of the first questions that every entrepreneur must answer at some point in their business journey is WHY? Why have I chosen to do with my life at this time? Why not just get a job? Why must I be the one to do it? Why does it need to be done, at all? Whether we're offering a product or service, our why must be resoundingly clear to us.

What is the purpose of our business? And the earlier we answer this question, the better for us and our brand. Because every day, the journey of entrepreneurship will throw curves that will push one to the wall and a clear understanding of the purpose of one's business will always be a defense and inner push. Whether the challenge comes from naysayers or well wishers or even from our own mind, our purpose for going into that particular business will be a sure defense. If you believe that your business has no relevance whatsoever and is not solving any of the numerous needs in society, then it may be time to reconsider going further with it, unless perhaps it is a hobby and not a business.

When we have answered the question of why, then we are better positioned to tackle the other questions of What,

Whom, When, Where and How. What is our product/service? Who is our target market and competition? When do we plan to make profit? Where will we find our clients and customers? And how will we interact with these customers/clients and our products/services?

Competence is simply a mastery of oneself, one's products/services, clients, and processes.

If we have developed a good process that we are convinced would satisfy the desires of our customers and clients, profit is only a matter of implementation. Money is a reward for problem solved and value offered. So how do we plan to solve whatever problem or need we have identified in the life of our client/customer?

We should be careful not to allow a study of competition sideline us in any new venture. Is it good to study our competition? Yes. But sometimes it should be more to find lapses that our business can improve on than to find points of brand intimidation or mindless copying. We must dare to be innovative in our creativity. Innovation may copy, but should always improve upon the original.

So study and know yourself and your products, know your clients and customers, study the market, and have a strategy for market entry and dominance. And be confident to see it through, and humble enough to adjust whatever doesn't work in your entrepreneurial process.

Being competent doesn't equal being unrealistic or having an unprofitable business strategy. In the promise of competence, an entrepreneur must be careful not to allow over bearing clients/customers bulldoze her into making unrealistic and unprofitable promises.

We are in business to make money, and in the case of social entrepreneurship, to make positive impact as well. A business is not a charity and should not be run as such. If you find that your business gets great reviews and your customer base is growing rapidly but you make little or no profit at all, and have no strategy to leverage the goodwill into profit in the long run, then you may not be operating a competent business but a charity.

I remember reading somewhere that a business can choose between only 2 of the 3 major client needs and would be hard pressed to satisfy all three which are; speed of delivery, quality and affordability. This resonates deeply with me as a business woman.

Simply, the faster a client wants a great product or service, the more they should be willing to pay for it. And the more affordable they want a great product or service, the longer they should be willing to wait for it. And the faster they want an affordable product or service, the less quality they should be prepared to accept. We may have a hard time giving our clients a great product/service, at very affordable prices and within the sometimes ridiculous speed they demand.

Know this and know peace. Decide if you are a premium brand or a regular brand and tailor your brand promise accordingly.

One evening, I was casually scrolling through Facebook when I happened upon an interesting question from one of my mentees who had come to me from time to time for business counsel, she was at a crossroads on whether an improvement on her branding and consequent increase in her product rates would have an adverse or positive effect on her business. I quite enjoyed some of the comments shared, some were in favor of her improving branding and others were in favor of her playing it safe and keeping her business at a most affordable rate.

I get this question sometimes as it is a cogent dilemma for most startups. To buttress my point about choosing your brand promise accordingly, I will share a little about my own food business, McOlivia's Kitchen. I launched my food business at what some may consider exorbitant food rates but I still had clients, because I was careful to target the people who can afford my meals from the very beginning. As I scaled, our products became a bit more affordable but still had enough room to increase prices and maintain quality as the cost of production sometimes fluctuated upwards. My entry strategy was simple, leverage my social capital in the beginning and build from there. Granted, I had some good leverage from my success as an event host and TV/Radio Presenter so I started out as my own brand influencer. My staff strength was low in the beginning but in 2 years, we had business presence in 3 cities and, we were able to move to a physical restaurant space, scaling organically. This is just phase 2 in what I hope to someday make a franchise, and I have been careful to remain profitable even from day one.

If we sell at a ridiculously low profit margin, as an entry strategy, we leave ourselves little room to maintain quality when cost of production increases.

The people who buy our products without proper branding and at affordable rates are most likely not the people who will buy our products when they are properly branded and more expensive. As we scale, it may be important to be consistent in our target market and advertising, otherwise we may need to start a different kind of campaign for our new target market if we ever get cheaper or more expensive. Granted, time teaches every entrepreneur what the best strategy could have been but most times it is too late as the mistakes have already been made. So we can try our best to learn from other person's mistakes and advice ourselves accordingly. So, ask yourself, who is already doing what I hope to do in my business? How have they remained profitable over time? Do they have books or seminars or conferences I can access? Are they available to mentor me through the process?

A part of knowing yourself is asking, do I want to be financially free or do I want to have urgent security? Do I want to make money to eat today or am I building a brand that would be able to scale, withstand market forces and become a household name someday. The best part is that whatever answers you choose, you are right.

Knowing our business goal will help us avoid distractions and withstand criticism and irrelevant counsel. I have been both persons at different points in my entrepreneurial journey, the one who is building enough to eat and the one who is building for tomorrow, and have learned a lot being both persons too. I enjoy reading Robert Kiyosaki's Cashflow Quadrant, which was the first gift I asked my husband for and that he gave me on our very first date. In that book, Robert speaks about the Employee, the Self-employed, the Business owner and the Investor. He mentions that he wrote Cashflow Quadrant as a sequel to his best-selling book, Rich Dad, Poor Dad. When he shares about the different persons in each quadrant, he does it with humility and understanding, having grown up under the dual mentorship of his *Rich dad and Poor dad*, two men who found themselves at different levels of financial freedom, primarily because of their nature. So whether we are self-employed or business owners, we are justified in our own right as entrepreneurs and should always feel free to act accordingly.

But whatever we do, and whoever we are, we can do our best to avoid any seeming business models which seek to ensure that we do not profit in the short run and in the long run.

While you can volunteer with an existing business to get some relevant experience and build competence, books are probably the most affordable way to learn about business, so consider investing in a few good books (e-books or hard copies) in the areas you want to learn and improve in your business. Always be ready to answer the questions that matter for yourself and your business.

CONSISTENCY

My husband, and business development consultant, Ray Anyasi, often says that businesses don't die if the founders don't give up on them. I found it a hard saying initially but the more I studied businesses that have stood the test of time, I find that these are mostly businesses that were run by men and women who did not give up even when the going got tough. Sometimes, the doggedness of an entrepreneur can be mistaken for foolhardiness especially when everybody else is convinced that their business will never recover from an obvious setback.

In 1998, Apple was bankrupt and on the brink of collapse. It had lost over a billion dollars in revenue within a financial year. Then Steve Jobs returned with a revolutionary energy, launching products like iMac and iPod. Today, Apple is the most valuable company in the world. In 2005, Delta Airline was neck deep in debt to the tune of several billion dollars. The company just couldn't keep up with competitions like Jet Blue and Southwest. It was so bad that a bankruptcy judge had declared, "I had not heard anything that I will say remotely impressed me that you have the money, talent, or the thought that you could successfully reorganize in this case." perhaps that was the trigger they needed to provoke their business beast mode because they *successfully reorganized*, and today are back in business as a leading airline.

Again, a clear understanding of the purpose of one's business may help sustain her in this trying time. Have I ever wanted to give up on my businesses? YES. But every time I consider the proverbial light at the end of the tunnel, I am propelled to simply re-strategize and get back on it. Sometimes, it seems like the light is simply not visible from where I stand and at such times, I take a long break and even cry about it, but I do my best to never close shop completely. I am overwhelmed with gratitude simply reflecting back on my journey as an entrepreneur and seeing how many times I came pretty close to giving up, for different reasons, but never quite shut it all down. It was a bit easier to run a business before I became a mother than it has been with the added responsibility of my brand of involved motherhood, so it has been nothing short of a miracle, for me.

In March 2020, the same month my journey as a mediapreneur took a beautiful turn as I took on my first role as Executive Producer for my Wedding Reality TV Series, Real Bridesmaids of Africa, a national lock down was declared and weddings and other events were paused. Initially, we assumed the Covid 19 pandemic may not last for long but months later, it became clear that we were facing a peculiar time in our generation's history. All over the world, schools were shut down, airports were closed, and most businesses had to find ways to work from home or face extinction. Many businesses were forced to rethink their business strategy and in this time, technology and the Internet seemed to be the saving grace of most businesses which depended on online conference calls to stay connected as well as dispatch companies to move products to their clients and customers. But the event industry took a major hit, as most events became virtual or were canceled or postponed indefinitely.

I think I did more than just cry, I was heartbroken because my partners and I had invested good time and resources, had already begun production and even had more weddings lined up to feature within and outside the country. In this same time, my restaurant which I had only opened a month earlier was also forced to shut down and I went back to working from home. But for my event hosting and production gigs, there was no home to work from, because events just weren't happening in that capacity anymore. For several moments, I toyed with the idea of letting the nearly 3 years of planning and back-and-forth emailing and brainstorming sessions it took to get a team in place and get some of the necessary equipment for production go down the drain. I was close to just cutting my costs and letting it go and quite understandably, but after a few months of soul-searching and re-strategizing retreats, I found the strength to pick up and bring an entirely different twist to the project that was definitely a better strategy and content than we earlier had, my partners loved it and more than a year after we shot our first 7 episodes, we were back on set again. This time, putting all contingencies in place even while knowing that life generally is unpredictable, but as long as we keep hope alive in our hearts, we will make our dreams come to pass.

So, I know that consistency is one of the biggest reasons why one business gives up in their 10th year, amidst uncertainties and another business goes on to succeed in their 11th year under the same circumstances. Adjust if you must, reduce staff strength where necessary, take business breaks whenever you need to, but never ever let hope die. Never ever give up on your vision and your business. I know this is easier said than done, as consistency has been one of the biggest issues of entrepreneurship, but I am convinced that one day, if we never give up, our sweat, work and tears will be worth it.

COLLABORATION

We live and do business in interesting times, where brand visibility, positioning, as well as market share is made even wider, more volatile by a common access to the global market as made possible by the Internet. The world of commerce, as we know it, has been reduced to a global village by the Internet, and when an entrepreneur leverages these strategically, the financial and other rewards for her business can be staggering. For this reason, I consider the Internet the biggest business collaborator of the 21st century. The depth of this collaboration is aptly captured by one of the founding fathers of the Internet, Bill Gates, in his book, Business at the Speed of Thought. In the chapter titled, Change the Boundaries of Business, Bill Gates writes;

"A flow of digital information changes the way people and organizations work and the way commerce is conducted across organizational boundaries. Internet technologies also will change the boundaries of organizations of all sizes. In changing the boundaries, the web 'workstyle' of using digital tools and processes enables both organizations and individuals to redefine their roles.

A corporation can use the Internet to work seamlessly with professionals such as lawyers and accountants who remain 'outside' the corporate walls as consultants rather than as company employees. An important re-engineering principle is that companies should focus on their core competencies and outsource everything else. The Internet allows a company to focus far more than in the past by changing which employees work within the walls and which work outside in an adjunct, consulting, or partnering role. Our core competencies at Microsoft are creating high volume software products, working with other software companies, and providing customer service and support. We outsource a number of functions that don't fall into those categories from help-desk technical support for our employees to the physical production of our software packages."

I believe these two paragraphs do great justice to my own sentiments and persuasions about business collaborations and the Internet. It is also note-worthy that Bill Gates' recommendations and practice builds largely on a clear understanding of the core competencies of his business, Microsoft. If we first understand the WHY of our business, then the subject of collaboration becomes an easier conversation. As we discuss the concept of collaboration between equally established brands, startups and established brands and between startups, let us lean more on collaborations between startups and established brands. This is because I have been a mediator between such brands in the past and at one point or the other, I have been a startup collaborating with an established brand and at other points I have been the established brand collaborating with a startup.

It is sometimes easy to assume that in collaboration between a big brand and a smaller brand, the big brand gives more and the small brand profits more, an assumption that is as easy as it is often erroneous. This knowledge will help you as a small business to approach bigger brands with equal confidence and humility. Confidence because you fully understand your core competencies and what you bring to the collaboration table, and humility, because you are the under-dog in the arrangement. A confident yet humble approach is such a powerful double-edged sword that it often slays any hindrances in the way of such collaboration.

But we are only able to position our brands to the extent that we are aware of such opportunities for collaboration. The principles that worked for me in my collaborative efforts with fashion brands and others, early on in my business sojourn, even before I had duly registered my businesses or put many structures in place, are the principles of service, mutual respect, regard for mutual benefit, contentment, networking and several sprinkles of bravery, matched with a willingness to give without always expecting anything in return. I try to be deliberate about building relationships, in business and in life, and I have found that most of my successful business collaborations come naturally from such relationships. For instance, I have collaborated with dispatch companies in Lagos and Abuja cities for my food business, and we have joined hands to deliver foods in the most unlikely times, during a global pandemic, and during large food exhibitions. Did I turn into a dispatch company when lots of other business owners began to inquire about my innovative and speedy delivery strategies? No? I was always careful to direct all dispatch business interests to my collaborative partner. A win-win for my business and for theirs, because we each stayed true to the terms of our core competencies and collaborative agreement. I believe some persons may turn down collaboration opportunities simply because they have been hurt in their past attempts and hoodwinked by their greedy partners in the collaboration. But I also believe that if we develop a reputation for being honest in our business, we would always have that goodwill to trade in collaborations. So let our business be reputed for good service and fairness in partnerships, as that goes a long way towards our social capital, arguably the best capital for collaborations.

Sometimes, there is also the initial curiosity and question of credibility for a small business, but this is where an outline of our core competencies backed up by verifiable consistency comes to the rescue. We may collaborate with any brand, big or small, as long as we have identified a point of mutual benefit and are clear on the deliverables of each party. We should never despise the days of our humble beginnings, because every big brand once had an early beginning where someone took a chance on them.

If you reach out for collaboration and get a rejection, consider it an opportunity to rework your proposal and reconsider the brands that you reach out to. Not everybody can collaborate with you, but if you look closely enough, you will often find someone who is willing to do great things with you, even in small ways. Take that chance and be great at it. More doors will open for collaboration.

4.3 THE HOME MANAGER WOMAN

Every woman can be a home manager, even though, more and more recently, most women are shying away from the responsibilities of managing a home. The most culpable reason is that the woman does not belong in the kitchen anymore but in the forefront of society, alongside the man, making things happen, and effecting what is termed as 'Relevant' Change in society. While I do not dispute the fact that a woman's training does not end in the kitchen, I also suppose this is an erroneous interpretation of the woman as a Home Manager, which forgets to put into consideration that the family is the smallest unit of any society and therefore a relevant building block of every society. Home management, in this instance, is not only about doing the job, but about getting the job done. So a woman who is a home manager is not only the woman who spends all her time grinding pepper, doing laundry or repetitively doing the same tasks over and over without proper planning and wearing herself out in the process just to answer the title of Home Manager.

No. Even though this is the most basic form of home management, it has evolved beyond that to accommodate the innovation and realities of the present day woman. Much like running a business, the home manager is a person in charge of the administrative aspects of a home, and is concerned primarily with effectively running the home, employing processes like planning, execution and controlling.

The home manager concerns herself with the hows, the whys and the whens of everyday living in the household. Issues like taking care of children, planning and making meals available for the family, ensuring the home is clean, personal and family hygiene, procurement of household goods, employment, training and management of domestic staff, budgeting and administering of the household finances, etc, are her primary concerns. In this way, the home manager can be a full-time housewife, or a work-from-home mother, or a business executive or the World Bank president. Whatever her role in society may be, the home manager understands that her job in her immediate family is an even greater service to humanity and the society at large.

Most of the challenges we face in our society today and the vices we work hard to curtail and eliminate daily are a reflection of the failures of families. So, when a woman rises up to the role of Home Manager, she is investing in the next generation and ensuring that the future is brighter and the society is safer, at least wherever her off-springs step foot.

Because the woman of the 21st century is educated and empowered, she has other responsibilities outside her home, so it is of utmost importance that she finds a way to navigate the issue of administration in her home with practical tested and trusted strategies. Some of these strategies may include;

4.4 PRIORITIZATION

To prioritize, in this respect, is to ask oneself, what is the most important and what is the least important. Personally, I had to make a list of the things that matter most to me in my home. The ones that are important and sensitive, I decided that I must try to always be the one to undertake, while the ones that are important but less sensitive, I delegate and supervise others. This is one way to save ourselves time and the stress of being worn out by every little task in our home. Here's a list of some tasks in the home on an everyday basis, you may enjoy listing these out and adding your own home tasks and drawing up a priority list. I have created this list in the order of the tasks I perceive to be most important and sensitive to the tasks I perceive to be important but can be delegated, depending on the peculiar needs of my family, my personal schedule, my spouse's schedule, number of domestic and voluntary help, age and number of children, and family budget. So for me, my priority list may look something like;

1. Family Nutrition

2. Family Hygiene

3. Family Rest and Relaxation

Structures and Systems for Family Nutrition

The basic and perhaps most recurrent task in the home surround food and nutrition. However, when broken into simple processes, there is room for delegation. In order of priority, family nutrition can include the following tasks;

> **Meal Planning:** I suppose that this is the core of family nutrition, where the nutritional needs of the individual family members is put into consideration. A task I am happy to do, sometimes consulting with a nutritionist. You can employ the services of a family nutritionist to decide what your family nutritional needs are and plan your family meals around that. For more on meal planning, please refer to chapter 3 of this book.

> **Meal Timetable (weekly or monthly):** This is one task that I do not necessarily enjoy doing but which is of great importance. I know how to draw up meal timetables but it can be a mentally tasking process, so sometimes I make several meal timetables and shuffle them such that month three timetable may just be a repetition of month 1 timetable, that way, I save myself the stress of repetition. However you prefer to go about it, a meal timetable is a great time-saver.

> **Budgeting and Drawing Up Grocery Shopping Lists:** While the woman must not be the one to provide the funds for family nutrition, a good home manager is more effective if she understands how to draw up a budget considering the funds available. She decides what foodstuffs are best bought in bulk like dry grains, and which ones are best left to weekly shopping like fresh vegetables.

- **Cooking:** I love to cook, and I know how to cook most meals. But that doesn't mean that anytime the gas is on, I am in the kitchen. When it comes to cooking, it is widely believed that this is a survival skill that everyone must possess but do not be embarrassed if you don't know how to cook, start with the easiest of recipes and learn, but if you do not love to cook, then try to be in a place where you can afford to hire the services of a chef or you can outsource the cooking once you know your family nutritional needs. One of my favorite tasks is drawing up simple recipes and pasting on the kitchen fridge so that at first glance anybody who has seen me prepare that meal can make a palatable version of it. I prefer to prepare the more complex meals like native soups but pretty much anybody old enough to be in the kitchen can boil rice or make eba or microwave food or boil eggs or blanch vegetables for salad. Interestingly, there are meals that I prefer my husband to prepare because his tastes better. Once we have trained anyone on how to prepare a meal, and the art of meal plaiting, we can give them room to prepare that meal, even when we are home and simply relaxing in bed. This way, we have time to do other things without jeopardizing our family nutrition.

- **Meal Prepping:** Anybody can cut vegetables and blend tomatoes if they are old enough. So while meal prepping is an important task for effective family nutrition, we can happily delegate this responsibility whenever we have someone available to do it.

- **Grocery Shopping:** Once the best markets and sources of different groceries are identified, pretty much anybody can do the shopping. The home manager saves precious time and can use this time as she pleases, even to get extra sleep or watch her favorite movie. I enjoy food shopping but I am careful not to wear myself out with tasks that can be delegated.

> **Doing the Dishes and Cleaning Up:** This is usually the final step after every meal time. Growing up, this task fell to the children mostly and I will be honest to admit that I did not enjoy doing the dishes because the sink was taller than me and I had to climb a kitchen stool to use it. Oh, and I just did not like it even when the water was made warm and a make-shift sink was stationed on the floor of the kitchen for my use. As an adult, I am indifferent and a little more tolerant of doing dishes. But I am more than happy to delegate this task to anybody available. I dream of the day my children will be old enough, so I can permanently delegate this task as part of their loving home training to become responsible members of society.

Structures and Systems for Family Hygiene

Tasks that concern family hygiene are second only to Nutrition, in my opinion.

> **Personal Grooming:** As women, It is important to be deliberate about personal grooming like taking proper baths, brushing the teeth, washing the hair etc to keep the body clean and prevent body odour. When this task is not properly learned in childhood, we are presented with adult members of society who go about stinking up the place. We meet them in different places, at the supermarkets, the banking hall etc. For this reason, a home manager should take particular interest in making this task serious for herself and younger members of her family like her children. Unlike family nutrition, where there is an immediate response of hunger and anger when meals are unavailable, the effects of poor personal grooming may be delayed

and show up much later in life and may be more difficult to tackle then

Washing, Ironing and Folding Laundry And Shoes: After deciding the frequency of washing clothes, we may feel free to delegate this responsibility to able hands. We may employ the services of a dry-cleaner or a live-in help, choosing perhaps to take care of our underwear personally. The invention of washing machines has made this once arduous task easier and less time consuming. So, if we do decide to wash clothes ourselves, we can be smart about the process. Same goes for ironing, folding laundry and cleaning shoes. Whether we use a laundry service or employ a help to do the laundry or personally do it, we may choose to have one day of the week assigned to folding laundry and placing in its designated place, making sure there are enough clothes for the week or 5 days at least. Personally, my wardrobes are divided into different categories like work clothes, gym clothes, church clothes, event clothes, jackets, pants and denims, underwear and casual home clothes which are mostly shorts and tank tops because a girl loves to look good at home. You can have a main wardrobe and a clothes organizer to help you decide once and for all, what clothes are needed for the week so that you do not spend your mental and physically energy making that decision each morning. This typically helps us avoid clutter and indecision, as living perpetually in a cluttered and disorganized space can affect us adversely and dampen our mood and sense of self-worth. We can even make this into a fun family activity with our husbands and children or siblings, once in a while. Having a wardrobe and clothes hangers is sometimes a function of space available, and finances but whether we have a big walk-in closet or a few bags to store our clothes, we can add a touch of our femininity to it by folding them neatly and applying our creativity to the management of our space. This gives such an energizing feeling when we look around our living space and find that all our clothing are clean, folded and in order, it can be both refreshing and empowering.

Sweeping and Vacuuming: A clean environment makes for a happy home manager. I learned a neat trick from one of my friends whose home always looks tidy, even with children. She cleans at night when the day is over so she starts off her new day with a clean home and her toddlers are more inclined to arrange whatever they scatter during the day. But hey, we have to be kind enough to ourselves to admit that our homes may not be tidy all day, especially when we have children and that is okay. We just keep doing our best at all times.

Structures and Systems for Family Rest and Relaxation

The home manager is an event planner automatically, whether she employs the services of a professional or she does the work herself, she is the one who decides that a birthday is coming up and a party is due, or that the family deserves some time out at the beach or a mini-vacation. I absolutely enjoy this task, especially because I suspect that I am the most outgoing person in my family. More often than not, my husband is happy to go along with my many plans for family rest and relaxation, as long as they are within reasonable budget and align with the family schedule. Sometimes I am also happy to fund such family outings in my exciting role as the family event planner. Birthdays, family reunions, spa treats, swimming time, and other fun hangout opportunities are an essential but often overlooked aspect of family time. As simple as family movie night or storytelling under the moon can seem, it can be as much fun for the parents as it is for the children. I enjoyed some good playtime with my siblings and parents as a child, so I am careful to recreate such wonderful opportunities for my family, irrespective of the city we find ourselves in. Children need to play, rest and relax, and so do adults because as the popular saying goes; all work and no play makes Jill a dull girl. Rest and Relaxation is discussed further in Chapter 6.

Bonus; Family Devotion.

I have included this family task here as a bonus because it should be an integral aspect of our daily life on our path to holistic living. Though I consider family devotion to **be of utmost importance**, after all a family that prays together does stay together, I suppose it is the responsibility of the spiritual head of the home. So far, it has worked out for my family as we have gotten into a habit of family prayer and bible study. Under different circumstances, a woman may choose to place this as her number one priority if she considers it her own responsibility for certain reasons. So family retreats and spiritual conferences can be at the discretion of the spiritual head of the home.

4.5 DELEGATION

As a home manager, a woman can employ others to help in the administration of the home. These may include paid or volunteer staff, as well as willing relatives like grandma and grandpa, cousins and siblings or even her husband and children, depending on their availability and her management style. But irrespective of the terms of this agreement to help, every woman must polish the simple yet powerful skill of delegation, to allow her the necessary room to groom her staff/helpers and enjoy more personal time.

Effective delegation can sometimes take many forms and can include some of the following steps;

1. Training: You train the person on how to perform the task you wish to delegate, do not delegate duties you haven't provided training for. You may train personally or outsource the training to qualified agencies.

2. Supervision: You supervise as they do what they are trained on, giving room for possible mistakes and correcting where necessary.

3. Mastery: You allow them to do it unsupervised and see if they have mastered it. If yes, move to step 4 and if no, revert to step 1 or 2 depending on the error level.

4. Auto-delegation: Once they get it right, please allow them the liberty to practice what you have taught them, and don't spend all your energy shutting them down or being overly critical of their service. Human beings have a tendency to give their best when they sense that we believe in their abilities, it calls out the best in them and allows them to grow. While a toxic environment and complaints can make even the most skilled worker fumble as a result of the confusion and chaos. So the calmer and more appreciative we are, the more likely to get the best out of our delegated helpers including our own husband and children.

5. Personal Freedom: Enjoy your new found freedom. Once you have effectively delegated a task whether it is folding of laundry, making of breakfast, cleaning of the fridge, disposing of refuse, ironing of clothes or washing of the bathroom, you can bask in the freedom of time saved and focus your energy on other matters within or outside your home, including but not limited to study time, hobby time, spa time, sleep time, vacation time, prayer time, girl time or career time. You can, as the old Igbo proverb goes, drink water and drop cup. In all these, we must let go of our perfectionist tendencies acknowledging to self that nobody may ever do it like we do it but being confident that they can do it in an acceptable way. If you want it done perfectly, do it yourself while the rest of us will be chilling on the weekends and you're stuck cleaning the stove because you won't just get out of your own way and let anybody help you. Or you can just let go and let someone else try to help you.

6. Inspection, Appraisal and Reward: Occasionally Inspect, appraise and reward excellent service. We can delegate a duty to someone and still watch out for how they're faring from time to time, just to be sure that they aren't becoming lax or cutting corners, or struggling in that duty. Sometimes a little expression of gratitude can go a long way when someone helps us. And even if we're paying someone to do a job for us, a simple "Thank You, You're doing a great job," can go beyond ensuring good service to assuring their loyalty. I found a book in my mum's library growing up, and while I found some of the content of it funny and others mischievous, there's this particular topic I have found useful. T. Scott Gross, in this book, How To Get What You Want From Almost Anybody, discusses the art of tipping and opines that one may sometimes tip in advance anticipation of a good service, tip proportionately or generously, depending on the dexterity required in delivering that service. He goes ahead to share a personal experience in what he terms 'The No-Tip Tip' which I find interesting.

"A tip doesn't have to be cash. Effective tips are often no more than a kind word or, in some cases, a clever word.

We were trying to hurry through the supermarket one busy Saturday and were doing fine until it came time to check out. All lanes were open and full so I cruised the registers until I found the checker with the most sign of life out of a crew that gave the appearances of having been rode hard and put up wet (a horse term for you city folks).

Working to the front of the line, I leaped close and said, 'we've been watching you, and you're really fast!'

I smiled, returned to my place in line and enjoyed the show as our checker put on quite a display just to prove my point."

The furthest step is rewarding excellent service. My domestic staff sometimes look forward to a monthly bonus, because it is not a fixed amount like their salary but a token reward as my appreciation of their service. And even when I never had any domestic staff, I have found verbal gratitude and a simple gift to open doors in people's hearts that make them desire to give us their best always. Like an extra cupcake for my daughter when she helps pour water in my cup or a thundering round of applause when she removes our plates after eating. Sometimes a little shift in our attitude to helpers is the main thing that would make us finally begin to enjoy the dividends of delegation.

4.6 OPTIMIZATION

Optimization Tools for a Home Manager.

An aspect of Work optimization for a woman who is a Home Manager involves having recurrent lists and processes readily available to maximize time and for effective management of her domestic staff and other available help. To avoid unnecessary and avoidable repetitive activities, and for effective budgeting and checks and balances, consider keeping copies of the following on your mobile device or relevant apps. And where necessary, keep physical copies on To-do boards around the home so that everybody in the home has the information relevant to them.

- Monthly or Weekly Meal Timetable.

- Meal Recipes.

- Grocery Shopping Lists.

- Daily/Weekly/Monthly To-Do lists.

- Appointment or Activity Reminders.

- Monthly or Annual Rest and Relaxation Planner.

- Weekly or Monthly Family Budgets.

4.7 WORK-LIFE INTEGRATION

This entire book is concerned with how a woman can safely integrate her entire life in a way that allows her to function in her different capacities whether as wife, mother, entrepreneur or career woman with enough time, energy and resources left to enjoy the fun things of life. So, that a woman is a home manager who doubles as a stay-at-home mother doesn't automatically mean she has more time on her hands for rest and relaxation than the woman who is a home manager but also doubles as a sales clerk. The reverse is also the case.

Having a functional social life is not a function of a woman's workload but is a result of a deliberate effort at planning, prioritizing and delegating aspects of that work load. So while I have read several intelligent articles on creating a work-life balance, I am inclined to prefer work-life integration, where work and life are happening simultaneously. When rest, good nutrition, relaxation, exercise and healthy relationships are made a deliberate part of a woman's everyday lifestyle, alongside work, then that balance is achieved which ultimately results in an integrated lifestyle.

Plan to enjoy healthy meal options whether you're at work or at home. Sometimes, this may require you to pack a fruit bowl or healthy snacks on your way to the office but it is important for your general well-being.

Don't have enough time to exercise? Consider parking your car or alighting from the vehicle a few blocks from your office and taking a walk the rest of the way to your office, or even taking the stairs instead of the elevator whenever possible.

Minimize burnout by taking short breaks as often as necessary and longer time-outs and vacations to allow you unwind and experience full relaxation of body and soul. An extra raise is important at work, but an unpaid leave to reset your mind and redeem your body is even more important when you feel the onset of work-related burnout. Simply unplug, refresh and restart. Embrace teamwork to ease the burden and collaborate whenever necessary. Delegate tasks whenever possible and normalize being a mother, even around work colleagues. Do not shy away from involving your children or spouse in your daily work live whenever possible. My daughter, husband and I enjoy synchronizing our calendar as often as possible and taking work trips outside our city together so that we can enjoy some mini family vacation time after the work is over. We travel together, my husband or I do the work we came for, and then we take some days off to unwind in the new city and come back home feeling both work-effective and rejuvenated. This is my own ideal picture of an integrated work life.

Before we get to the end of this book, I am hopeful that we would have a much clearer road-map towards work-life integration as a key to holistic living for women. So let us forge on.

I'm excited to be on this journey with you, queen.

"A strong woman understands that the gifts such as logic, decisiveness, and strength are just as feminine as intuition and emotional connection. She values and uses all of her gifts."

– Nancy Ratburn.

CHAPTER 5
EXERCISE

Pam woke up with a loud ringing in her ears. Her body was a bit sore to touch because she had finally joined a fitness class with her *bestie* in their bid to court the attention of Adjoa, Buogo's rich new Ghanaian neighbor. The fitness instructor had said not to take any painkillers for the soreness and to give it a few days so her body can adjust. For some reason, Buogo seemed to be taking it quite well and had no complains about body aches. Pamela had confronted the instructor with that comparison and he assured her that different people respond to a new exercise routine in different ways depending on their lifestyle and body type. She was not going to continue arguing like a cry baby so she was giving exercise a few more chances like everybody had encouraged.

Pam had come home late and hidden in her own room from all the noise and attention in the house. Everybody wanted a piece of her; from her very needy husband, who she was happy to get away from, to the twins who were crankier than her first child ever was. Edna was her only safe place in that home. Sweet Edna, with her big beautiful eyes and constant smile. They were renovating the house and somehow the landscapers were being very noisy with their equipment.

A knock came on the door, it was sharp and loud, everything was loud lately. She was just about ready to tell her husband to take it easy with the knocking when the door creaked slightly and opened widely to reveal her first daughter, Edna.

"Oh," she managed a little smile now and somehow the headache seemed bearable as she pushed away the duvet and motioned Edna to join her in bed. This little *munchkin* made her day brighter any day anytime.

"Did you sleep well Mummy?"

"Yes, my darling. Thanks for asking."

"You're welcome, mummy. Good morning. Why are you holding your head that way? Are you hungry?"

"My head hurts a bit, my love. The traffic last night was terrible. And yes, I am famished."

"Great, daddy sent me to call you because breakfast is ready. We made your favorite."

"Oh yum, which of my favorites?"

"Pancakes, scrambled eggs and smoothie."

Pam beamed with a wide smile as she picked Edna up from the bed and planted her feet firmly on the floor. They raced to the kitchen to join the rest of the family for a hearty breakfast. Pam couldn't resist flashing looks at her husband. There was something different about him this morning. He was shirtless and somehow seemed a bit more masculine and well toned. She felt a bit of attraction rise in her and she calmly shook it off.

After giving birth to her twins, she didn't quite understand how her libido disappeared. It had been nearly a year since, and she still found his many sexual advances a huge bother. But today something was different. Maybe it was the fact that he looked really good shirtless or perhaps it was the dates in the smoothie. Whatever the reason, she had a feeling that she wasn't going to work early today. Thank goodness, her younger sister was on break from school now, and could take care of the twins. Once Edna left for school, she was determined to take her husband to their room and find out why his mere presence was making her feel warm all over.

****

My friend, who is a nutritionist, called me one evening to point out that my dress looked ill-fitted in a picture I had posted online, and we talked briefly about my BMI (Body Mass Index). Turns out I had put on some weight due to work related stress and I wasn't quite ready to lose the weight. I was eager to follow a workout routine and was convinced that all I needed was an accountability partner, and I would get my summer body ready. A few months and one accountability partner later, I was still eating whatever I could find and satisfying my sugar rush with fizzy drinks. I had just gone through a major health issue, so I wasn't even in the right frame of mind to entertain any naysayers. I had a hard time looking in the mirror and one day, someone dared to compare me with his wife and advise that I lose weight like his wife. *Na God save am that day,* because it took all my home training to rein in my tongue and act composed. People are often careless and say the meanest things to us as women concerning our weight, not caring where we are emotionally and mentally, and even the private battles we face that lead to what they see outwardly. They are often so quick to condemn.

Next time we are tempted to point out that another woman is fat or skinny, we should bite our cheek instead, and if we must speak, it should be to ask her how she is and compliment her for being alive. For a girl who was a late bloomer and had no noticeable breasts or buttocks as a teenager and early adult, I was actually happy when I got married and had my daughter and started to flourish in certain areas of my body. But almost immediately, those same people who taunted me for being skinny, turned around to advise me to *'take it easy'* when I started to put on flesh. What many people don't realize is how proud I am of my curves and every inch of my body, because every part of my body tells a story.

As women, the shapes and sizes of our body parts are all deliberate to support our life journey.

I can't even recall how many times I've gotten away with certain things or fit into certain age-groups simply because I am petite in size.

Before we begin to worry about our body weight and losing weight, let us consider what is considered healthy weight.

5.1 BMI

Just because we can't fit into our friend's size 10 dress or our old clothes, doesn't mean we are unhealthy or fat. If your weight is a source of constant worry, you may consider taking a break from watching too many TV commercials with size 0 models and bodies that may have been surgically enhanced, or ingesting every advertised weight loss pill. Let's talk about BMI and the weight range that is healthy for every woman.

Body Mass Index, or BMI, is a measure of body size. It combines a person's weight with their height, thus.

BMI = Weight (Kilogram)/Height (Meter squared)

BMI = Kg/M2

According to author Derek Llewelyn-Jones in his Gynecological best-seller, Everywoman,

"The first thing to remember is that there is no 'ideal' body weight. There is a preferred body weight range; it is preferred because if your weight lies in this range, you are less likely to develop high blood pressure, diabetes and some other illnesses. However, these weights may not be accurate for some women, such as those who are very active or who come from certain cultural backgrounds."

He continues, "If your BMI lies in the 19-24.9 range, it is in the preferred range for health and appearance; if it lies in the 25-29.9 range you are overweight and may consider losing weight by increasing your exercise and choosing a weight-reducing diet. If your BMI is 30 or more, you are obese."

5.2 THE JOURNEY TO A PREFERRED WEIGHT

Thank God that my Health and Physical education teacher in secondary school made a show of teaching us about the different body types; endomorphs, ectomorphs and mesomorphs, and the peculiarities and strengths associated with each body type. That helped me appreciate my body to an extent and just marvel at what it could do and discover sports that I was better suited for early on. Every week from my primary to secondary school, we had a day we would go outdoors for physical education (PE), and just have fun playing different games and trying out new sports activities. In primary school, it was games like jumping rope, playing ten-ten, football and dancing games. I was the lead bass player in my school band and we matched during morning assemblies and often travelled to represent our school in these extracurricular functions. In secondary school, I was an excellent sprinter and average cross country runner, as well as an amazing discus thrower. I didn't do so well in Long jump but it didn't stop me from entering for long jump competitions even if I come out last, I did it for the fun of the game.

In retrospect, I realize my childhood and teenage years were filled with lots of fun outdoor activities and social exercises. And I suspect that it is same for a lot of us as women. By university time however, most of us lose that streak of freedom and fun found in physical activities, games and sports. Maybe because in the university, it is not a mandatory requirement for graduation or perhaps it is the more subtle reason of our new found femininity and need to appear unruffled and always prim and proper. All valid excuses. But by the time we leave university and begin to take on adult roles either as full time workers, mothers and wives, we find that we have less and less time for physical fitness. As valid as our reasons may be, it is even a far bigger tragedy.

The older we get, the less time we may have for exercise, but it is true that the older we get, the more exercise we may actually need to keep our body, soul and spirit working well. By default, children hardly sit in one place, from climbing furniture to jumping on beds and running five errands at a time, their life is naturally filled with many runs as they have very little care in the world, a spring in their feet and a lot of sugar in their diet. So even without meaning to, their lifestyle already incorporates a lot of physical exercises. As adults, our lives are marked with lots of sitting around in front of a desk or in front of the TV, partly because of our job descriptions and partly because of our self-restrictive leisure options.

Beyond physical fitness, exercise does wonders for our mental health and can improve our mood and productivity to a large extent as women. This is due to the hormones released during exercise. There are even some simple exercises that help during pregnancy and menstruation to ease cramps. I was pretty impressed when

I learned of these and will always remember my pregnancy yoga days with all fondness. As a mother, it becomes increasingly difficult to maintain a healthy sex drive and libido, but exercise is one good way to restore the body to its youthful state and get it to engage in and enjoy sexual activities even after childbirth.

In this chapter, we explore the different benefits of incorporating exercise into our daily lives as a key to holistic living for women, and these rewards range from physical fitness to desired physique, emotional and mental well-being, as well as sexual satisfaction and mindfulness.

So whether we're trying to lose weight, gain weight, get pregnant, become a better sex partner, tighten certain body parts, gain confidence, stay positive or balance our BMI (Body Mass Index) to stay healthy, there are different forms of exercise that can help on our fitness journey.

5.3 FORMS OF EXERCISE

There are many different forms of exercise tailored towards helping the body build one of four things, which include Endurance, Balance, Flexibility or Strength. Some exercises can help in more than one area. While some persons prefer to focus on just one form of exercise, a blend of all four types on different levels can be of most impact toward our general fitness.

Endurance

Endurance exercises are more commonly referred to as aerobics, and they include activities that increase our breathing and heart rate. Generally, endurance exercises, when done right and consistently, keep our heart, lungs, and circulatory system healthy while improving our total fitness. My favorite exercises are endurance exercises. Anything that increases my heart rate and breathing, I find exciting and you may often find me at the forefront. I am not surprised about that because I was a cross country runner, as a teenage student, and I have always enjoyed dancing.

While they may seem difficult at first, most endurance exercises typically get easier with time and even make everyday activities easier for us, so we don't end up panting profusely after climbing a few flight of stairs or chasing our toddlers round the house when we become moms. Physical exercises that build endurance include;

DANCING: I recently joined a dance class to learn Salsa, Zumba, and master some contemporary moves and it has been as rewarding socially as it has been for my physical fitness. Dancing leaves me feeling so free. It is a rhythmic exercise that packs so much fun. I enjoy dancing so much, that one period I was feeling particularly low and I told my gym instructor so. The next time I came to gym class, he walked up to me and explained he was switching up my entire aerobics class and we were doing a dance choreography routine instead. He had noticed me dancing randomly during short breaks in our aerobics classes so he figured I might enjoy a full dance class to get me out of the blues. And boy, was he right. Those were the best two hours I'd ever spent in that gym. I had more fun than a kid in a candy store, and I just let my body lead me in liberating moves.

At the end of that fitness dance class, I had worked up such a sweat and I felt way better than I did in days. So yes, dance is a powerful form of exercise and quite honestly the most entertaining exercise if you ask me. The best part about dancing is that you don't need to go to a dance studio for it. You can play your favorite songs on your phone or blasting through the stereo, or if you're anything like me, you can put your favorite FM station in your car and dance in your parking lot. I dance at every slightest excuse and opportunity, and even in church, I've sort of become known for being the excited woman that dances energetically during praise time. So much so that one day, a lady in the choir walked up to my husband, Ray, to ask how I was doing and to say the choir has missed my dancing that Sunday. We had sat in another part of the congregation and you couldn't see me dancing if you were seated at the choir stand. Wow, I blushed a bit when Ray told me someone had asked about me and missed my dancing.

Beyond its endurance benefits, dancing can help build coordination and flexibility, as well as improve our confidence and self esteem. It has helped me make friends in the most unlikely circumstances, and yes, if you're looking to meet new people, consider joining a dance community, you're guaranteed to meet friendly people who are open to new friendships while dancing. And bonus point, some beautiful relationships are only born when we step out of our home to actually interact with others in this big beautiful world. So, we .can create time within the week to go dancing, perhaps one hour after a long day at work, we can just take time off to go cool off and dance at a social spot around the office or closer to home,. You may be amazed how much you would enjoy it. I have had a fun time inviting some of my friends out to dance and I am yet to meet anybody that did not enjoy the time spent dancing. There's no judgment on the dance floor. As you find self expression on the dance floor, you get to be your true self through dance. Oh, we may stay forever young at heart and look forever sweet 16 if we make dancing a part of our lifestyle.

SWIMMING: Swimming is a form of low-impact exercise that can build both cardiovascular and muscular strength. However, it requires a high level of endurance and uses more muscles than other forms of aerobic exercise, especially the abdominal and gluteal muscles. This makes swimming a good way to lose belly fat and tone the body generally.

Every time we perform an endurance exercise, our brain releases endorphins which are the body's natural pain reliever and feel-good hormone. I believe this is one reason why we feel so excited after a great work out. I would catch myself singing gently in the shower at the swimming pool after I've spent time swimming, I used to wonder if people could hear me but now I don't care much because I know most people at the swimming pool and they really don't care. But even if they did care, we all paid equally for access to the facilities at the swimming pool so I might as well sing in the shower, even if I miss a line or I'm off-key from time to time.

CYCLING: When we incorporate exercise into our lifestyle, it becomes easier to be consistent and enjoy its lifelong impact. Cycling is a great way to build endurance while going on simple errands like grocery shopping. And yes, expect a few falls when learning how to ride a bicycle if you never learned it as a child. True story, I didn't quite learn how to ride a bicycle even though my older brother had one while we were growing up, it just always seemed so risky. I was already a mother when I mentioned to my husband that I had never rode a bicycle and would you believe it, we were off to buy a bicycle the very next Monday and ended up with two bicycles, one for me and one for our daughter. Beyond endurance, cycling helps me build balance and I still blush whenever I remember how people stared and some even clapped in encouragement or plain surprise that day as I rode my bicycle home, struggling so hard to maintain balance and just making a show of dragging it home. People wonder why a grown woman couldn't ride a bicycle but I am more than excited to be learning at this age. So whether you know how to ride a bicycle or not, you're not too late to learn this fun and endurance exercise. Don't forget to wear your helmet when riding a bicycle.

CLIMBING STAIRS OR HILLS: We can turn this everyday activity into a deliberate workout. Even at the gym, the trainer has a good time giving us stair climbing targets. If we have to climb the stairs 10 times, it usually starts off like an interesting easy-peasy flow, until somewhere around the third round where our feet would typically start to feel heavy, especially if we overestimated our stamina and started off running on the stairs. This is the one sure place where slow and steady does win the race. Depending on what you hope to achieve, you are likely to last longer if you take it easy. But do not go at a snail-pace, a moderate pace is enough to get your heart thumping and keep you energized enough to go the whole 10 rounds, or more or less, depending on your target.

PLAYING TENNIS, FOOTBALL, OR BASKETBALL: A team sport that is considered fun by most people, the duration spent playing tennis, football or basketball counts a lot towards our endurance activities for the week. Personally, I prefer to team up with fellow women and play against other women in any team sport, because men are just built differently from women. As long as I have not joined the major leagues, I am happy playing at my speed and with people my own gender and at my level. The goal is to build endurance, and not to win at the game. If you ever wish to play with men, be sure that the boundaries are clearly understood to avoid injury. Pay attention to your body, stop if you're feeling dizziness, chest pain or pressure, or any discomfort. And get the necessary rest and help.

BRISK WALKING OR JOGGING: Whether we're going on a stroll with a loved one or an early morning jog, the secret is to maintain a pace that keeps our heart rate going. A brisk walk is slightly faster than the usual leisurely walk and a jog is even more so. Experts suggest that a jogging pace is generally between 4–6 mph (6.4–9.7 km/h), while a running pace is faster than 6 mph (9.7 km/h). I try to listen to music when I go on a jog and this serves as great company. If we are lucky to find a partner to go on a jog with, then we're in for a jolly exercise but if not, we can be content with playing our favorite songs on our headphones while doing this endurance exercise. A good pair of appropriate shoes support the body and are excellent for brisk walking or jogging. Also, we are better served if we wear comfortable and light clothing and only follow routes that we know and that are safe.

HOUSE WORK LIKE VACUUMING AND MOWING THE LAWN: Yup! Turn chore-time into workout-time. Not every day wear a long face while mowing the lawn, sometimes put on some music and enjoy the exercise. Your body will thank you for the workout. We're practically killing two birds with one stone when we do certain house work that doubles as exercise. Chores like Vacuuming and mowing the lawn are good ways to build endurance in your body. An attitude change towards this otherwise mundane task can quickly transform this into an enjoyable workout routine, if we just give it a try and think positive.

JUMPING ROPE: This is probably one of my earliest introductions to endurance cardio workouts. As young as primary school children, we jumped ropes during break time and our rope was nothing sophisticated, made from rubber bands stringed together or long tree ropes from our school orchard. It was all fun and we incorporated lots of singing to this enjoyable exercise. Today, there are all sorts of ropes with advanced features that even help us count our jumps. If one has an old or new injury on the feet, it is advisable to take a break from jumping rope to avoid wearing out the muscles. Whether you use an old-school rope or an advanced rope, make sure you're jumping. Even without a rope, you can still do an imaginary jump and the benefits are almost similar. They include; Well toned calves, a tightened core, improved lung capacity, Improved Stamina and general body fitness. Jumping rope is also a great way to lose weight.

Strength

The second form of exercise we discuss are exercises for Strength, often referred to as strength training or resistance training. Strength training helps to build up our muscles. Strong muscles and bones assist our posture and are great for carrying out everyday tasks like carrying groceries and lifting toddlers and even all the kneeling and standing involved in gardening. Strengthening the muscles also stimulates bone growth, lowers blood sugar and reduces stress and pain in the lower back and joints.

We tend to lose muscle mass as we grow older so strength exercises can help build it back and make us less likely to fall. We can choose to use equipment like dumbbells or weight machines, but we can also choose to use our own body weight as resistance while working out. One of the biggest advantages of strength training is that it can help us lose weight and this is because resistance training helps us lose fat while still building muscle and this is great for our body metabolism. Some exercise for strength or resistance training typically include body weight exercises like squats, lunges and planks or exercises involving resistance from a weight, a resistance band, stretchy elastic bands or a weight machine. They include;

LIFTING WEIGHTS: It is funny when people say that weight lifting is not for women and makes women look like men. While it is funny, it is quite understandable and grossly untrue. Depending on the body size and weight, there are appropriate weight sizes that can give one a trim look and help you lose weight. But you have to consult with your trainer to recommend appropriate sizes for you. Start with lighter weights and build up from there. The first time I tried lifting weights, I realized that it wasn't as scary as I used to think and ever since then, it has taken a lot for my fitness instructor to discourage me from carrying weights that are practically beyond my range per time. But I am learning to calm down and take it easy and I'm enjoying the effects of weight lifting. Apart from the physical effects, lifting weights helps a woman build confidence knowing that she can hold her own if she ever faces a bully.

LUNGES: Lunges help to challenge our balance and improve functional movement in so doing. The muscles in our leg and glutes (buttocks) benefit most when we do lunges. Firm thighs can be an exciting reward after this otherwise difficult training exercise. Personally, I love to do lunges in front of a mirror, maybe because I love how I look and I just like to appreciate myself while putting in the work for my summer body. If you're adding one or two dumbbells to your lunge routine, consider doing fewer sets especially as a beginner.

ABC of lunges;

- Begin with your feet and shoulder-width apart and put your arms down at your sides.

- Using your right leg, take a step forward and bend your right knee at the same time, stopping once your thigh is parallel to the ground. Do not extend your right knee beyond your right foot.

- Push up off your right foot and return to the starting position. Repeat this process with your left leg.

End. Repeat for as many rounds as required.

SQUATS: Squats are a good way to improve your lower body and core strength, as well as flexibility in your lower hips and back. They are a great way to lose weight and tone the buttocks generally too. Resistance bands are pretty affordable and we can use them in our squats for maximum effects.

ABC of Squats;

- Begin in a standing position, with your feet slightly wider than shoulder-width apart, and keep your arms firmly beside you.

- Next, chin up and chest out, as you gently push your hips back and bend your knees like someone about to sit in a chair.

- Be sure not to bow the knees inwardly or outwardly, and ensure your arms are in a comfortable position.

- Bend until your thighs are parallel to the ground, take a short one-second break, then extend your legs and return to the beginning position.

End. Repeat for as many rounds as required.

PLANKS: Planks are an effective way to build core strength and stability and improved balance in our day-to-day activities. They help to tone both the abdominal muscles as well as the entire body. Beyond just burning fat around the abdomen area, planking helps to tighten the tummy. Unlike sit-ups and crunches, planks stabilize our core without straining our back so much. I especially love planks because they help to stretch my back after a long day wearing heels. As planking works to lengthen our hamstring and the arches of our feet, it is considered a dual strength and stretch exercise.

ABC of Planks;

- Get on your hands and toes, as if you're in a push-up position with, your back straight, and your core tight.

- Ensure your chin is slightly tucked and your gaze just in front of your hands.

- Make sure that you are taking deep controlled breaths while maintaining tension throughout your entire body, so your abs, shoulders, triceps, glutes and quads are all engaged.

End. Repeat for as many reps and sets as required.

It isn't always advisable to stay in the plank position for too long as more doesn't always equal better. A 30 seconds plank may be enough and you can take a break to catch your breath and repeat for three or more sets as you desire. If you feel any unusual pain or notice that you're getting out of form while planking, please take a break.

Flexibility

How often do we bend down to pick up something and feel so rusty getting back up? That is usually an indication that we need flexibility exercises. As children and teenagers, we have very little care in the world as we run around and do the most unthinkable back flips but the older we get as women, the more we lose flexibility in our tendons and muscles which can lead to an increase in the instances of muscle cramps and pain, as well as strains and joint paints. The primary objective of flexibility exercise is to stretch our muscles, as stretching helps maintain flexibility, and improves range of motion, posture as well as breathing and circulation. If we often feel stress in our muscles, then a simple stretch exercise can help reduce muscle tension and soreness ultimately restoring flexibility in that part of our body.

While stretching exercises do not give the rush that endurance and strength exercises may give, research suggests they are very important to protect the muscles from pain and injury which can result if we continue to do other forms of exercises or daily activities that contracts the muscles (shortening them), without doing flexibility exercises to stretch those muscles (lengthening them), returning them to full capacity and offering us a better range of motion to enhance our other forms of exercises and our daily lifestyle.

At my aerobics and dance classes, the trainers would often encourage us to stretch our muscles after the exercises to help our body get into a more flexible state with some touch-your-toes, hands-on-your-neighbors-shoulder, head flexing and simple yoga poses. Stretching can help lower cortisol levels and would generally make us relax after a workout routine. It is true that stretches are easy and simple exercises but it is best to do a little warm up before stretching to allow for improved blood flow to the muscles and therefore reduce risk of muscle injury. If we add a simple massage right after our stretches, then we improve our chances of a really good sleep after the exercise routine. I do this when I have had a hectic week and just want to rest my entire body during sleep. This is my recipe for a baby-girl-for-life nap.

Exercise + stretch + massage = Baby-girl-for-life nap.

We will discuss more on rest and relaxation in Chapter 6 of this book.

So let's get stretching ladies.

Some simple flexibility exercises;

KNEES TO CHEST: This exercise stretches the muscles of the lower back and glutes (buttocks). And can be completed within 30 seconds to 2 minutes. You would need only a yoga or other workout mat.

How to;

Step 1: Lie on your back and gently pull your knees into your chest using your two hands.

Step 2: Keep your lower back on the floor.

Duration: Hold the posture for 30 seconds to 2 minutes. Take a break anytime it becomes too difficult.

SIDE STRETCH: This exercise stretches and strengthens the intercostal muscles, these are the muscles found between the ribs that help support the ribs.

How To:

Step 1: Stand with your feet hip-width apart and clasp your hands above your head.

Step 2: Gently lean your body to one side, feeling a deep stretch along the side of your body.

Duration: Hold for 10-15 seconds and repeat on the other side.

STANDING QUAD STRETCH

This exercise stretches the muscles on the quadriceps, that is the front-thigh muscles. We can do it once we wake up from sleep or after a workout routine. Please take care with the standing quad stretch if you're prone to knee or lower-back pain.

How to:

Step 1: For balance, stand upright next to a wall for support if necessary.

Step 2: Keep your feet hip-width apart. Reach back and grab your right foot using your right hand.

Step 4: Keep your thighs lined up next to each other and your right leg in line with your hip. Feel the stretch in your right thigh and hips. Repeat with your left leg.

STANDING HAMSTRING STRETCH

This exercise stretches the neck, calves, hamstrings, glutes and back. It can be completed within 45 seconds to 2 minutes. We would need only a yoga or other workout mat.

How to:

Step 1: Extend your left leg out by placing the heel on a raised surface like a log or a stair.

Step 2: As you bend at the hip, ensure that your spine is straight, and bring your chest towards your thigh.

Step 3: Your right leg which is not being stretched will also bend gently at your knee-area.

Duration: For maximum impact, hold the hamstring stretch for about 10 to 30 seconds. Disengage if you are faced with persisting pain.

Balance

Balance exercises are important for both young and old women. Understandably, the older a woman gets, the more she typically needs balance. This is because as women age, our vision, inner ear, leg muscles and joints, which are the system that help us maintain balance, begin to break down. Studies suggest this balance decline begins around age 40 and 50 years. The National Institute of Health in the United States reports that one in three people over 65 will experience a fall each year and 1.6 million older adults go to the emergency room each year because of these falls. That's an alarming rate of falls which sometimes result in bruises, fractures and broken bones.

Thankfully, balance exercises can effectively reduce and sometimes reverse the rate of this breakdown, ultimately restoring balance and preventing falls in women of all ages.

The reason most women will buy heels and not rock them, only admiring them as they waste away in their wardrobes is because they're afraid of falling. No matter our age, if we usually fall, or are often afraid of falling and would like to regain confidence and feel steadier on our feet, we may consider doing balance exercises that keep us moving our feet on the ground. Even when we don't have balance problems, prevention is mostly safer than cure so we can start now to do some simple balance exercises, such as;

1. Standing on one foot for a short period of time and switching to the other foot.

2. Sitting down in a chair and standing up especially, without holding onto anything.

3. Yoga. Yoga is essential for building balance and even helps in building muscle strength which makes it an excellent exercise routine. Most yoga poses help burn calories, and in addition can teach mindfulness.

5.4 DEPRESSION VS EXERCISE

The book Everywoman: a gynaecological guide for life, shares some great insights for women's health and in the chapter on The Things That Happen to Women, author Derek Llewelyn-Jones shed a little light on depression in women. He writes, *"At all ages of life, women are more likely to develop depression than men. Most people feel miserable or have the blues at some stage of their life, and this is normal. Depression is less common, but can be serious. Clinical depression is associated with changes in brain chemistry. Twice as many women as men have an episode of depression sometime in their life. The reasons for this difference are not clear. It may be that in our culture, women are permitted to show emotion and have changes in mood, whilst men are not and consequently are more likely to deal with emotional problems by anger, aggression, violence, or the use of alcohol."*

Men can get depressed and women can get depressed, and pretty much everybody has had a bad day at some point or another. What some people label as depression may simply just be sadness or a bad hair-day or a broke period. So, before we rush and label ourselves or others as depressed, we can be kind enough to get an expert opinion so we don't just rush off mislabeling ourselves and others. Thankfully, women are expressive in our society today and we can always try talking to a friend or loved one first when we're sad or after a bad day. I wish that somehow we can find a way to get the men around us to open up and share some of their challenges and then help them. Our society encourages men to act brave, and hide their emotions, even when opening up can be the very thing that saves us all on most bad days.

In the wake of the COVID19 pandemic, there have been increased reports of depression and anxiety, and understandably so, because of the many uncertainties, and overall health scares, as well as loss of jobs, friendships and loved ones.

All over the media, there is such a panic frenzy that at some point, I had to shut off news channels just to maintain my personal peace and breathe. Yes, we need to know what is going on in the world around us but if we ever feel harassed by the bad news in the media, it is okay to take a break and catch our breath. We can take as many breaks as possible, not only from the media but from anything that seeks to steal our joy and peace. I have also heard personal reports from other women on my shows about experiencing different levels of fear and panic in these times. It is commendable that some individuals and corporate bodies as well as governments and non-governmental agencies have teamed up to provide access to therapy in these times. While some persons may freely take advantage of this solution, some other women may not be so fortunate for several reasons.

For one, issues concerning emotional and mental health are still largely misunderstood and are mixed up in several misconceptions, so our society has not yet come to terms with the realities of this aspect of health care. There is still a level of stigma surrounding depression and anxiety so most women still have a hard time identifying and coming to terms with their personal struggles and seeking help. Again, even when a woman is brave enough to seek the help she needs, the services of therapists have been reported to be costlier than most women can afford. So what can a woman who has no access to therapy do anyway for her emotional and mental well-being?

I believe exercise can be one such easy, accessible and affordable way to get the spring back in our steps and push the blues away. But be sure to get medical advice from your doctor or other qualified clinician for any serious health conditions.

According to Harvard Health, exercise is an all-natural treatment to fight depression. Dr Michael Craig Miller, assistant professor of Psychiatry at Harvard Medical School suggests that exercise works as well as antidepressants in mild cases thus, "*For some people it works as well as antidepressants, although exercise alone isn't enough for someone with severe depression.*"

"*In people who are depressed, neuroscientists have noticed that the hippocampus in the brain—the region that helps regulate mood—is smaller. Exercise supports nerve cell growth in the hippocampus, improving nerve cell connections, which helps relieve depression,*" explains Dr. Miller.

So now we know the power in working out, I hope we push away every reluctance that stands in our way and put one step in front of the other as we begin our journey towards exercise and freedom. Listen, nobody ever said it would be easy but focus on your goal, and keep in mind that there are millions of women all over the world who wake up just like you each day and choose to give life another shot and just do it. You can start with dance or jumping up to your favorite song, or you can start with running a short distance one morning and then the next, or talking a short walk in the evening, or simply start with stretches in front of the mirror. Whatever you do, understand that you are showing up for yourself and that matters more than anything else. The rewards may be slow but if you don't give up, it will be worth it.

It would be even more commendable if individuals and corporate bodies as well as governments and non-governmental agencies can provide more opportunities for women to network and exercise as a way to stay physically fit and mentally alert, through fitness hubs, standardized gym centers, dance events, etc. The approach has to be both sustainable and adapted to the culture of the people to be effective. Women in this part of the world love to dance and connect with each other, opportunities for such may prove most effective and an easy-to-track solution. I played around with the idea of a social workout spot right in my home and invited a few neighbors to join in and dance and work out. We had no professional trainer, but we had lots of fun and a few good laughs with our simple equipment like skipping ropes, resistance bands, bicycle and music box. I imagine that it would be a lot more effective if this kind of social fitness is replicated in different communities and at different levels. Would you be willing to try it? It might be fun and may be a way to meet new friends and socialize while burning fat and staying healthy and happy.

5.5 A WOMAN'S SEXUALITY

Most women enjoy sex but in our society, a lot of these women are shamed into pretending that they do not enjoy sex for fear of being labeled as lose women even while married. Such women tend to be too shy to explore sex confidently with their spouses and therefore do not fully enjoy the benefits of sex in their marriage. They do not know how to give or receive sexual pleasure adequately.

It is interesting to note that some women even on their wedding night prefer the lights off on their matrimonial bed simply because they are both ashamed of their own bodies and they do not know how to go about sex with their spouses. Another group of women who sometimes do not enjoy sex are those who have given birth and find that after childbirth, certain parts of their body do not return to its original status and this leaves them with feelings of embarrassment and sexual inadequacy.

For every scar, stretch-mark and sag on a woman's body, there is underlying beauty and a compelling story, sometimes occasioned by childbirth and sometimes by the intricate design of life itself, so it is nothing to be ashamed of but a badge of honor to be celebrated. Whether we have perky or droopy breasts, big or small breasts, large or small waists, we are very unique and there's nobody quite like us anywhere in the world.

Thankfully, exercise has many benefits for a woman's sex life as shown by different studies on exercise-induced sexual arousal. A vigorous workout affects hormones, neurotransmitters and autonomic nervous system activity. It also raises and sustains levels of an enzyme in women that increases genital blood flow and arousal. One such study claims that 20 minutes of exercise could boost sexual arousal by 169%. This arousal effect persists for a short time in women, but is very possible. If you notice that this happens to you, then you may maximize that knowledge by scheduling a great session with your husband just after your exercise.

I have been privileged to enjoy the many benefits of exercise as it concerns sexual intimacy from the earliest months of my marriage and even during my pregnancy. Because I engaged in pregnancy workout, I was able to maintain a healthy sex drive for the most part of my pregnancy period. But as sexually expressive and physically fit as I was, it was humbling to find that having a child did reduce my sexual dexterity at first. It was frustrating to find that my sex drive was gone as well as my previous sexual abilities. However, at my sixth month postpartum doctor's appointment, my doctor finally agreed that I had healed well enough and approved my return to exercise and in that moment, I knew the game was about to change in my favor.

As I went back to my exercise routines, my stamina was greatly boosted and this led to an increased endurance as well as strength to enjoy enhanced sex drive for longer stretches of time. Suddenly I was better in bed after having a child than I was before. How did this happen, you might wonder. The answer is simply targeted exercise.

There should be no shame in enjoying a healthy sexual life within the happy confines of a loving marriage, before and after having children. Your doctor should advise the best time for you to begin exercising after having a child, this duration differs in women just as our body and healing differs.

Here are some simple exercises that can help restore our body, rebuild our confidence and reawaken the lover in us for a more sexually satisfactory experience in our marriage.

Exercises for Improved Sexual Performance and Enjoyment in Women. No Equipment Necessary.

LUNGES

We already learned that Lunges boost flexibility, so this workout will not only help firm the muscles in your leg, thighs, hips and buttocks, giving you the stamina, strength and endurance you need during sex but will also make it easier for your husband to access your G-spot in almost any position.

How to do Lunges in 4 easy step.

Step 1: Place your feet hip-width apart and put your arms down at your sides.

Step 2: With your back straight, take one step forward using your right leg, and bend your right knee at the same time, stopping once your thigh is parallel to the ground. Let your right knee be directly above your right foot.

Step 3: Hold for 20 to 30 seconds, then slowly push your right foot back to the starting position.

Step 4: Repeat this process with your left leg.

End. Repeat for as many reps and sets as desired.

SQUATS

Squats are a good way to improve our lower body and core strength, as well as flexibility in our lower hips and back. They strengthen our lower and upper-leg muscles and the glutes. If you're ever on top during sex, you'll be grateful for the level of control and endurance you get from squats.

How to do squats in 4 easy steps

Step 1: Stand upright, with your feet slightly wider than shoulder-width apart, and your arms firmly beside you.

Step 2: Chin up and chest out, as you gently push your hips back and bend your knees like someone about to sit in a chair.

Step 3: Bend until your thighs are parallel to the ground, (the lower you go the more you work your gluteus maximus, which help you to extend and laterally rotate the hip joint. Do not bow your knees inwardly or outwardly.

Step 4: Pause and relax, slowly pushing up from your heels as you return to the starting position.

End. Repeat for as many times as desired.

PELVIC LIFTS

Pelvic lifts strengthen our glutes (muscles in our buttocks) as well as our lower abdominal muscles, which we tend to use most during sex. Majority of us sometimes complain of pain in the lower back and this can make sex a painful task. Pelvic lifts straighten the lower back and help build core strength which can give a woman all the drive she needs to enjoy sex in different positions as she pleases. If you are ready to maneuver your husband during sex and show him a new improved version of you in the bedroom, then pelvic lifts will empower you with the skills you need.

How to do Pelvic Lifts in 4 easy steps

Step 1: Lie on your back facing the ceiling, with your knees bent and feet flat on the floor, shoulder-width apart.

Step 2: Lift your pelvis such that your spine is in a straight line.

Step 3: Squeeze your abs and the muscles of your buttocks (glutes). As you do this, push your inner thighs towards each other. Stay in this position for 5 to 15 seconds.

Step 4: Relax and lower your buttocks to the floor again.

CARDIO

Not only are Cardio exercises good for our heart, they're also amazing for our sex life. If we wish to enjoy improved stamina and an improved blood flow and increased chances of an orgasm, then we should focus on those exercises that get our heart pumping. Such exercises like running, whether on a treadmill or outdoors, cycling, and swimming can do one a world of good in the bedroom. If we can get 30 to 60 minutes of cardio exercise 2 to 5 times in a week, we may notice the astonishing improvements in our sex lives. If we do this long enough, we may conquer the fear that comes whenever we consider being on top. Feel free to explore the sex positions that leave you feeling empowered.

KEGELS

Kegel exercises have become increasingly popular for men as well as women whenever the conversation of *sexercise* comes up. It is such a subtle exercise yet packed with so much value for the pelvic floor muscles, especially the *pubococcygeus* (PC) muscle. As we perform kegels, we strengthen our PCM (*pubococcygeus* muscle), which are the muscles that contract during an orgasm.

Research has shown that constant kegel exercises can help make the vagina tighter, and potentially lead to more intense orgasms. This doesn't surprise me because a part of enjoying mind-blowing orgasm is knowing how to pace oneself during an orgasm.

The best part is that Kegels are so simple that we can do them anywhere and at anytime. At work, during our lunch break, in the car, and every where we can think of.

How to do Kegel Exercises in 3 easy steps

Step 1: Contract your pelvic muscle just as if you're stopping the flow of urine, squeezing it tightly as if you want to lift it up.

Step 2: Hold in that position for 5 to 20 seconds, but be sure to maintain regular breathing.

Step 3: Release your pelvic muscles. Then repeat the process 10 to 20 times in a row.

You can do this simple kegel exercise 3 to 5 times daily for maximum results. The better you get at it, the longer you can hold each contraction. You got this, queen.

5.6 FLAT TUMMY WORKOUT

The older we get, the more difficult it may be to fit into our favorite pants or dresses, and while weight gain is an issue that concerns both men and women in our society, women often seem to be the worst hit, partly because of child-bearing and partly because we tend to be more self-conscious about our body. There are health concerns associated with excess body fat, which make it a smart health decision for a woman to keep excess fat away as she gets older.

Fat is stored in the body as essential, subcutaneous or visceral fat. Visceral fat or belly fat is the white fat that's stored in the abdomen and around all of the major organs, such as the liver, kidneys, pancreas, intestines, and heart.

High visceral fat levels can increase one's risk for heart diseases, high cholesterol, type 2 diabetes and high blood pressure.

So, any exercise that helps us increase muscle mass, and burn off excess belly fat is going to help restore our youthful waistline eventually.

Even if you're slim, you still need to be careful to keep your visceral fat low to reduce your risk for related diseases.

Here are some exercise that we can incorporate into our lifestyle for a flat tummy and a healthier body.

ABDOMINAL EXERCISES

Abdominal exercises tackle belly fat to give a well toned stomach. Whether at home or at the gym, alone or in a group, these exercise can help to give one a trim body.

PLANKS

Planks make use of the arms, legs, and all of your abs, making them an all-round and efficient way to exercise.

How to do planks in 3 easy steps

Step 1: Get on your hands and toes, as if you're in a pushup position with, your back straight and your core tight.

Step 2: Ensure your chin is slightly tucked and your gaze just in front of your hands.

Step 3: Ensure that you are taking deep controlled breaths while maintaining tension throughout your entire body, so your abs, shoulders, triceps, glutes and quads are all engaged.

End. Repeat for as many reps and sets as required.

Don't stay in the plank position for too long as more doesn't always equal better. A 30 seconds plank may be enough and you can take a break to catch your breath and repeat for 3 or more sets as you desire. If you feel any unusual pain or notice that you're getting out of form while planking, please take a break.

LEG LOWERING:

Leg lifts and leg lowering can be better than doing crunches, because we are putting less stress on our vertebrae when we do them.

Step 1: Lie on your back, place your arms firmly beside you, with your legs straight and together, and lift both legs up so that your two feet are facing the ceiling.

Step 2: While keeping both leg in that position, gently lower one of the legs straight down, as close to the floor as possible, being careful not to hit the floor, and then return to the top.

Step 3: Alternate between the two legs for as many reps and sets as desired.

LEG LIFTS

How to Do Leg Lifts in 3 easy steps

Step 1: Lie on your back, keep your legs straight and together.

Step 2: Lift your legs all the way up towards the ceiling, till your buttocks slightly come off the floor.

Step 3: Lower your legs down slowly till they're just above the floor. Hold for a moment.

Raise your legs back up. Repeat.

HIIT OR INTERVAL TRAINING

HIIT is simply High-Intensity Interval Training and they are effective for burning belly fat because they mix in short periods of intense exercise with lower intensity moves and allows one some time to rest in-between.

The trick is to target one exercise real quick, for like 30 seconds, take a break and then do the next one in quick succession for another 30 seconds. You will be left feeling breathless, for sure, but the energy burst and the rest in-between may keep you excited enough to continue going. I am not a big fan but perhaps with time I may change my mind.

Some HIIT exercise you can try include burpees, jumping jacks, jump squats and high knees. Beyond just burning belly fat, most of these exercises work to help you lose weight all round. However they require a great level of dexterity and caution, so be sure to consult with a fitness trainer or check for videos online for your first attempt of these exercises. Once you get a hang of them, I hear they can be quite fun and practically breathtaking.

AEROBIC EXERCISES

Find an aerobic exercise that you love and commit to a 15 to 30 minute workout daily to burn off excess fat in your tummy. Some easy aerobic exercises include running, swimming and cycling. If you cannot make out time daily for aerobics, then try to find one day in the week to do at least 1 hour of aerobics. You can use the facilities at the gym or find a workout partner to stay accountable and keep you motivated.

Worthy to Note

Here are a few safety precautions we can keep in mind when exercising, especially as a beginner.

1. Remember to KISS (Keep it short and simple). 30 minutes of exercise is okay in a day, so we should avoid the temptation of over-exercising. If we start off too hard, there is a risk that we will give up easily. So, better ease into it. Also, there is a tendency for the body to produce excess cortisol when we over-exercise. Excess cortisol can make it even more difficult to lose belly fat. So let us take it easy and trust that slow and steady will give us the desired waistline.

2. Stay hydrated while exercising. Let us remember to drink water as we work out and our body loses some of its fluids as sweat.

3. Remember to breathe regularly.

4. If we are uncomfortable or unsure of any exercise, we should consult with a doctor or physiotherapist first, especially in the case of injury.

5. Stay alert. If we're exercising outdoors, please stay within safe areas and be aware of our environment.

6. Smile often. You are not under any punishment so take a moment to smile and appreciate yourself for taking care of yourself. You got this, queen.

Factors to Keep in Mind on a Weight-loss Journey.

Now that you know which exercises are good for you, and you may have decided to embark on a weight loss journey, here are some factors to keep in mind to eliminate disappointments and release you from unnecessary pressure, in order to ensure that your fitness journey is both honest and realistic.

1. Weight loss is not a linear process. If you notice that you lose weight quicker when you first started on your weight-loss journey than you do now, don't panic. It is all normal.

2. Make fitness a part of your lifestyle. The faster you lose weight, the more likely you are to gain it back, so take it easy. Experts recommend losing 1–3 pounds (0.5–1.36 kg), or approximately 1% of your body weight, per week, to avoid muscle loss and increased chances of irregular periods, headache and dehydration. The aim is to make it a part of our new lifestyle and not just something we do and then stop after 3 months when we get to our ideal weight and shape. We need to make fitness a lifestyle to get in shape, and stay healthy.

3. Maintain a healthy Diet. No matter how hard you work out, please bear in mind that a balanced nutritious meal is also a key part of your fitness journey. Weight loss occurs only when you burn more calories than you consume.

4. Your genes may affect your jean-size. It is true. Studies have shown that genetics play a role in weight. So as much as you aspire to lose weight, also consider whose daughter you are and let your expectations be tailored accordingly. Knowledge is power, and this knowledge can make you be kind to yourself and stop comparing your fitness journey to others.

5. High-intensity exercise releases the body's feel-good chemicals called endorphins, resulting in the "runner's high" that we experience when running or jogging. However, low-intensity exercise sustained over time encourages the release of proteins called neurotrophic or growth factors, which cause nerve cells to grow and make new connections. The improvement in brain function makes us feel better. So depending on whether you are trying to lose weight real quick or improve your mood, exercise can sure help. Take it one day at a time.

With this in mind, here's a compilation of estimated weight loss rates, according to Harvard Health.

Estimated weight of individual: **155 pounds (70kg)**

Workout duration: **30 minutes**

ACTIVITY	CALORIES BURNT	ACTIVITY	CALORIES BURNT
Walking at a moderate pace of 4 mph (6.4 km/h).	167	Swimming in backstroke.	298
Jogging at a 5-mph (8-km/h) pace.	298	Swimming in breaststroke.	372
Jogging at 6-mph (9.7-km/h) pace.	372	Swimming in butterfly.	409
Cycling on a stationary bike at a moderate pace.	260	Swimming in treading water.	372
Riding a bicycle at a moderate pace of 12–13.9 mph (19–22.4 km/h).	298	Practising Yoga	149

So cheers to a fit lifestyle, and rocking the best outfits we've always dreamed of.

"Of course it's hard. It's supposed to be hard. If it were easy, everybody would do it. Hard is what makes it great."
– Tom Hanks (A League of Their Own).

CHAPTER 6
REST AND RELAXATION

10

9

8

7

6

5

4

3

2

1

Hurrayyyyyyy! Happy New Year!

The sound of firecrackers rang through the air as the New Year was ushered in. All around her, there was joy and celebration but Pam couldn't stop her heart from racing now. The loud outbursts and bright lights from the firecrackers had set her on edge and she felt ambushed.

A cold sweat broke out on her face. She had to get away from there and find some semblance of peace and quiet or she risked going into full blown panic attack right in front of their old and new friends who camped around the bonfire. Everybody was excited and seemed preoccupied in the celebrations. Even her husband who she had begun to enjoy some intimacy with in the past few weeks did not notice the fear and alarm in her eyes. She clutched her chest tight as all sorts of craziness flashed through her mind. And then almost in a flash, she made a run for their private quarters upstairs.

Nobody had seen her leave, or else how could she explain the silence she now heard. Even in the privacy of her own room, she was still panting as she felt herself sink lower onto the bathroom floor. This was the third time it was happening in the past 2 weeks, and somehow she had managed to hide her horror from everybody at work and at home. The fireworks went off again and this time louder and longer, and she clasped her head firmly in her hands. It was happening, her biggest nightmare was here and somehow she felt herself slipping away and losing control. She gave in to the overwhelming emotion and lay there in a pool of her own tears, rocking back and forth and finally wishing that somebody would find her even in that mess.

Somebody.

Anybody.

She was sobbing hysterically now, the tears from her eyes joining the catarrh from her nose and dripping down her face in an overwhelming mix of fear and self-pity. This seemed almost like dejavu, like she had been in this place before and felt this exact same feeling. Oh, now she remembered, it may have been a movie perhaps. Surely, it could never have been her and even now it seemed surreal. Was she losing her mind, or what was this tightening she felt in her chest?

She had never suspected that she was battling anxiety and yet here she lay, feeling both helpless and hopeless. She opened her mouth to say a prayer and no words came out, only soft trembling whimpers of surrender. In her heart she prayed for a miracle, and not just from this nightmare but from the horror that had become her life lately. She closed her eyes tightly to shut out the noise and bright light, but she could still feel her senses explode in loud bursts within.

And then it happened. A gentle tap on her shoulder jolted her and as she looked up, she saw what she felt must be the figure of an angel beckoning her. As the car sped out the driveway to the hospital, she opened her eyes enough to find it was her husband behind the wheels. It wasn't an angel after all.

****

While on family vacation at the Obudu Mountain Resort, we took a trip to the Holy Mountain, a picturesque place of prayer and history, where hundreds of mountains exist. The Nigeria-Cameroon border is in clear view from the mountain, and you see how magnificently the mini waterfall descends from the source. On our way back from the mountain, there was a heavy fog and we could barely see up to ten metres ahead on the scooter. So I was not prepared for the burst of emotions that hit me when we came upon a small settlement of local women and children gathered at the community tap, singing, playing and pouring water on each other as they waited turns to fetch water. It was such a nostalgic sight and as we sped further down the mountain, away from the natives, it took the threatening clouds for me not to ask our tour guide to stop me there so I could share in their joy and happiness.

These were a people of simple means and as much as we like to label them as underprivileged because of the lack of infrastructure and technological development in their communities, I consider them more privileged than some of the wealthier people I have met in my travels. They were rich in friendship and laughter, and there was scarcely any among them apparently anxious or depressed. Although they were not dressed in the finest of linens or designer clothes, and although they had no running water at home, they had gardens rich with local herbs and vegetables and they enjoyed the mild sun on their bare backs in that cold clime as they enjoyed each other's company. I longed for the joy that was carried in their laughter and envied the casual patience with which they sat and stood around the tap and had a good time *gisting* about their daily lives and sharing in each other's lives. They were going about their daily live but they were doing so in a most calm and relaxed manner.

6.1 REST

When we speak about rest, we often refer to any activity that puts our body at ease from work and expending energy. It goes beyond just sleep to include all periods of simply being, and not doing. Even when we lie down with our eyes evidently open but in a relaxed position of inaction, where we're doing absolutely nothing but daydreaming, then we may be said to be taking a form of physical rest. However, there is a place for sitting still and resting with a nice leisurely book and there is a place for deep sleep. All play vital roles in a woman's health and general well-being. So rest can be passive rest or active rest and can take many forms including social rest (time away from toxic activities and people), mental rest (time away from mentally challenging tasks), spiritual rest (time spent with your creator), or even sensory rest (time away from bright lights, noise and technology overload). Passive rest can include activities such as napping, and sleeping while active rest can include meditative exercise like yoga, taking a leisurely stroll, enjoying your favorite song or just daydreaming while lounging on your sofa. We need all these forms of rest at some point or the other in our day-to-day activities to stay sharp, energized and focused. The most recurrent and widely accepted form of rest however, is sleep.

Sleep

Cambridge dictionary defines Sleep as the resting state in which the body is not active and the mind is unconscious. There are five different stages of sleep and so to feel truly rested, refreshed and ready to take on a new day, a woman's sleep has to truly go through the stages. For instance, experts say that the body has to reach Stage four referred to as the healing stage, for tissue growth and repair to take place. This is the stage where important hormones are released to do their jobs, and cellular energy is restored.

Experts also recommend that adults should get about 7 to 9 hours of sleep every night. So a three hour sleep may feel like it's enough for us because we are trying to meet a work deadline but until we begin to prioritize sleep and respect ourselves and our body by getting adequate sleep each night, the healing work that takes place during sleep cannot happen. And yes, deadlines are good once in a while but we can't live our life perpetually on a deadline mode and not overwhelm our system someday. We have to take it easy, as we need all the rest we can get so that we continue to enjoy the full functions and reach the highest potential of our body and mind.

When a woman has a new baby, the new responsibilities sometimes make it harder for her to get enough sleep each night and this is counter-productive for the mother and child. I believe, that apart from the exclusive role of breastfeeding her child, every other task can be delegated to loving members of her family, friends or helpers. And even with breastfeeding, breast pumps have made it such that a woman can express her breast milk and have her partner or available help feed her baby whenever is necessary. So, if you're a new mum, resist the urge to do all the work that you are tempted to do, even if you feel agile and strong enough. Your body has done such a wonderful thing and you need time to allow your body heal and fully recover.

Push away every feeling of guilt as you deliberately find creative ways to sneak away and sleep till you've gotten the recommended dose of sleep for an adult. Having a child doesn't disqualify one as an adult and unfortunately, doesn't give us any super-powers so we still need to sleep like the rest of other humans to reduce irritability and other things associated with a lack of sleep. A well rested mother is good for baby and good for mummy and good for everyone, really, because nobody needs a cranky new mum and a cranky new baby on their hands. One of the biggest advice from most mothers to new mums is to sleep when the baby is sleeping, and as funny and cliché as that initially sounded to me, I am now inclined to accept it as practical advice. Once I deliberately accepted that it was possible, it was easier for me to simply relax my mind and whenever my daughter fell asleep, I do my best to sleep off too. Don't say it is impossible until you have truly made up your mind to try it, you'd be surprised how much sleep you may get when your child sleeps. Typically, new babies sleep way more than adults so be rest assured that once your baby is well fed and dry, he/she is most likely to sleep for long stretches at a time. Maximize this time, momma and get some sleep too. Any other house chores can wait until we are both awake. This is why we looked at delegation as an essential aspect of work in Chapter 4 of this book. Even a new mum is better served if she has someone she can trust enough to take care of her baby while she sleeps.

In countries where daylight savings are observed, sleep disruptions occur and can have some negative implications for the people who did not plan ahead of time to balance their sleep schedule during and after daylight savings. Even when I first moved from the east to the west within Nigeria, it took a while for me to adjust to the fact that the day typically ends later in Lagos than it used to in Enugu, partly because nighttime comes faster in the East and partly because the city of Lagos is the commercial hub of the country and people carry on with business beyond midnight. I had to advise myself of what time should be my bedtime, otherwise I stood the risk of being carried away by the lure of a city that hardly sleeps.

There are many factors that can affect a woman's sleep and one of the funniest yet somewhat terrifying reasons I've heard on my radio shows is an over-indulging sex life.

I am laughing thinking of the stories I've heard from women whose husbands just don't let them sleep at night because the children are in bed and they are excited to be alone. It can be cute until it becomes an intolerable routine that completely disrupts sleep time. Sadly, I haven't quite figured out a reasonable response to that. Perhaps consider taking work breaks and scheduling some afternoon _good time_ so you can both sleep better at night while still enjoying a healthy sex-life. Anything is possible with deliberate planning. It is as funny as it is a sensitive issue because constant sleep deprivation, even for the most mundane or good reasons can lead to some discomfort at varying degrees. This is because, according to experts, quality sleep is as needed as food and water when it comes to the issue of living a healthy life. Personally, I find that I am most creative and at my best behavior when I have enjoyed a good night sleep or afternoon nap. As a creative, sometimes I find that I may not be giving my best at work or experiencing a mental fatigue. On many occasions when this happens, I simply shutdown whatever I'm doing and go lie down for a power nap. More often than not, I wake up bursting fresh with ideas and ready to tackle the work with even more vigor and refreshing perspectives.

Let us do our best to eliminate whatever constantly causes us to lose sleep, whether these are real activities like late night work, time spent mindlessly browsing through social media, TV time or school work, and even perceived feelings of inadequacy. We must not make a habit of skipping sleep. Have you ever heard someone complain that they don't deserve to sleep yet because they haven't worked enough for the day? Yup, that someone used to be me some years ago, as well as several other women who haven't yet figured out that sleep is not a reward for work, sleep is what you owe your body for the wonderful work it is doing keeping you alive. And in the end, everybody pays that debt one way or the other. Ever heard of sleep debt?

Sleep Debt

There's this pretty cheesy thing we say in Nigeria, *everyday na for thief, one day na for owner of house,* which loosely implies that there's always a day of reckoning. So let's say that one has fallen into the habit of over-working herself because she's trying to win the award of wife of the year or mum of the year, or she refuses to leverage her teammates at work and instead hoards all the work to herself and even brings work home all in a bid to prove to her employer that she deserves the Employee of the Month cardboard plaque or she is constantly guilt-tripping herself into taking more orders from clients than she can safely deliver, so she is forced to stay up sewing till the wee hours of the morning every single weekend that she isn't at her 9-5 job. Or for instance she stays awake binge-watching all the seasons of GOT, and reading all the reviews she finds online for each episode, simply because she does not want to let go and accept that her failed relationship is finally over.

Girl, the body is taking note. And our body does not like this new habit. It is not in line with the baby girl lifestyle we promised ourselves and that we know we deserve.

Sleep deprivation can lead to mood changes, weight gain, trouble remembering things and concentrating, and even likely accidents resulting from drowsiness. When sleep deprivation becomes prolonged it can lead to even more serious health issues like a weakened immunity, high blood pressure, risk for diabetes, and early aging. In the case where sex is the excuse for constantly denying ourselves a good night sleep, we stand a risk of a reduced sex drive in the long run. Yup, we had better get that sleep now otherwise our body is going to just get fed up one day and revolt.

Work is good, family is beautiful, relationship is awesome, but we can never pour from an empty cup. We need to take such good care of ourselves that whenever we reach out to take care of someone or something else, we do it from a place of wholeness and deep personal fulfillment.

Sleep is so vital to life and yet so easily overlooked but when we don't get a proper night sleep, we owe our body a debt that incurs interest. That is to say that if we miss 3 hours of sleep today, we cannot repay it with 3 hours of sleep the next day, the body is a shrewd banker. When we miss sleep and try to catch up later, it takes extra time for our body to recover. According to a 2016 study from National Institutes of Health, it takes four days to fully recover from one hour of lost sleep. That's a lot of time to pay for whatever award we were trying to win at the expense of sleep. So, for what it is worth, we do ourselves a great disservice when we consciously and deliberately lose sleep. Unlike food, exercise and all the other things we consider important in life, all we need to sleep is to simply lie down and close our eyes, no special preparation or expenses required. Sleep is such a powerful yet free gift from a loving creator.

It's Payback Time

If for reasons beyond your control you realize that you have a sleep deficit and you want to pay this sleep debt back and get back to living your baby girl lifestyle without being so grumpy all the time, and to enjoy life at your utmost most creative self, then consider these suggestions from Ana Gotter, in an article in Healthline blog, medically reviewed by Debra Sullivan (PhD).

> - *Take a power nap of about 20 minutes in the early afternoon.*
> - *Sleep on the weekends, but not more than two hours past the normal time you wake up.*
> - *Sleep more for one or two nights.*
> - *Go to bed a little earlier the next night.*

The article suggests that if you experience chronic sleep debt, then you'll need to go a bit further to make some long-term changes. Changes may include;

> - *Go to sleep 15 minutes earlier each night until you reach your desired bedtime.*
> - *Don't sleep later than two hours past when you normally wake up, even on the weekends.*
> - *Keep electronics in a separate room.*
> - *Think over your evening routine to see if anything is keeping you up too late.*
> - *Stop using electronics two hours before bedtime.*
> - *Make sure your bedroom is dark and cool enough.*
> - *Avoid caffeine late at night.*

> *Exercise no later than three hours before you go to bed.*
> *Avoid naps outside of 20-minute power naps.*

In addition, I think it can help to use eye masks to block out lights if you find that light disturbs your sleep and also consider meditating at night to calm your mind just before bedtime.

As you finally settle into sleep, be sure that you are not just lying in bed for 7-8 hours, tossing and turning, but aim to get enough deep sleep too, so that your mind and body can feel refreshed when you wake up.

There are five stages of sleep that rotate between non-rapid eye movement (NREM) and rapid eye movement (REM) and include drowsiness, light sleep, moderate to deep sleep, deepest sleep, and dreaming. According to experts, deep sleep takes about 13 to 23 percent of sleep, which is about 62 to 110 minutes if you sleep for 8 hours a night. During deep sleep, a lot happens in the mind and body and it is in that time that the immune system is strengthened, the brain detoxifies, memories are consolidated, physical healing occurs in the body etc.

So if you realize that you toss and turn while sleeping every night, and wake up feeling tired or with constant headaches instead of feeling refreshed, then you may not be getting enough deep sleep. Consider speaking to a health practitioner to be sure that all is well with you. There is medical help available for different sleep disorders. Nothing should stand in the way of your good night sleep. When you start sleeping well and getting quality sleep, you may be pleasantly surprised to find out that all the while you used to mislabel yourself as short-tempered or easily irritable and feisty, you were just sleep-deprived.

The best part is that even the career and relationships that kept us up at night and we had to spend so much extra time working so hard at and getting small results would become an easy-peasy walk in the park, once we start approaching life from a rested point of view. It's time to Sleep and Slay, baby.

Those that called us names are about to change their testimony about us and call us peaceful and graceful and I'm here for that transformation.

No sleep + No work = Unproductivity

Little sleep + over work = Minimum Productivity

Normal Sleep + Normal work = Maximum Productivity + Slay!

6.2 RELAXATION

To relax is to be free from all stress, anxiety and worry. It is a state of enjoyment where one frees herself to receive the best treatment possible for the renewal and rejuvenation of self.

Every queen needs to relax and simply be taken care of. When we are deliberate about relaxation, we are acknowledging that we matter and we are worth the effort. On the surface, it may seem like relaxation is an unnecessary indulgence, to the untrained eye. But the modern woman knows that she did not come to this world to exist, pay bills, make impact and die.

NO!

Life is to be lived and enjoyed to the fullest. When we give ourselves a treat or allow ourselves be pampered, we are only acknowledging the good life that we deserve and honoring our highest self. Beyond taking a break to rest, relaxation is taking self-care to the next level and prioritizing your happiness and joy. It is simply putting you first without any self judgment, knowing fully-well that you are your own biggest support system and you need to show up for yourself so that others can learn how to treat you simply by observing how you treat yourself.

When I learnt to be deliberate about relaxation, it was a powerful game changer in my journey as a woman. Often times we assume that only the rich and wealthy can afford to relax but that is as disempowering as it is a false narrative. I agree 100 percent with wealth being a state of mind, to a very large degree. We can't have enough money to begin to prioritize practices like rest and relaxation. It isn't something money buys us, and it is achievable at most social levels if the consciousness and desire is imbibed from the start. Let us consider different forms of relaxation in the *'baby-girl'* lifestyle and how we can even afford to fund these. You've just *gotta* let go and enjoy yourself, *mamacita*.

Hobbies

The first question to answer in trying to figure out what relaxation options are available to one is, what is my hobby? A hobby is simply something that we enjoy to do, without any necessary promise of remuneration or reward. Simply, your hobby is something you like to do and can do, for free, and with very little persuasion. These days, I see that some of us tend to be political in what we acknowledge as our hobbies, only listing those things we feel may sound politically correct and appealing to a prospective employer on our resume or present us in *'wife material'* light or simply as cool gals. If we let anybody influence or bully us in everything else, we must not allow anybody bully us in what our hobby should be. Hobbies are allowed to be boring, or unsophisticated or even downright repetitive. So when it comes to hobbies, it is okay to choose something that we honestly find enjoyable and not something that we think our friends would approve.

There are many different types of hobbies to choose from and it is even okay to invent your own hobbies if you please.

From bird watching, to drawing, painting, make-up, graphic design, gardening, cooking, sculpting, singing, dancing, creating or solving puzzles, knitting, braiding, baking, traveling, blogging, acting, swimming etc. The range is limitless and quite invigorating when done in honesty. As long as your hobby is not a vice, and doesn't hurt anybody or break any laws, feel free to create time once in awhile to enjoy your hobby. And you don't have to be perfect at it to do it, it is not a job and you should not judge or pressure yourself when it comes to choosing a hobby. A hobby is something you do for yourself, just to reward yourself for being you.

There doesn't have to be any reasons for having a hobby and no qualifications required. Even my little daughter has a list of hobbies that started as early as before she was even a year old. That's if you count peek-a-boo and making faces. I do. Now she enjoys riding her bicycle, scratching puzzles, throwing ball, chasing chickens, and playing the guitar. She has a good time everyday doing one or more of these activities. Find what makes you happy, and be happy to do it as often as you can. Whatever you do, be careful to protect your hobby from unnecessary pressure. Sometimes people get so good at their hobby that others begin to pay them for it and they are happy to charge a fee. With time, they are left with one regular job, one hobby-turned-job and no time for relaxation and fun. This is an anomaly occasioned by lack of boundaries and sometimes poverty. Know your hobby and leave it at that. Whenever we decide to start charging a fee for our hobby, we risk losing the carefree, no pressure, freedom that the hobby used to give. Once you find this happening, please feel free to create another hobby for yourself, because money is important but relaxation is important as well.

Hangouts

Can we agree to normalize hanging out with the girls on the weekend, going to the salon together and maybe karaoke on Wednesday? Ladies night out used to be such a wonderful time but I fear it is now an endangered activity. With the rise of social media, there is an actual alarming decline in real life social hangouts. And yes, networking for business purposes is good, but I'm talking about the organic networking for the plain purpose of catching fun. As women, we have fun as single girls without a care in the world. But who made the silly rule that once we're married or become a mother; life has to become so serious that we can't spare a moment for a ladies night out or sleepover. If we have friends that are worth our time, it's time to schedule a spa-date or sleepover where we can be all girly and enjoy ourselves as women. If you have no friends who are worth your time, then it's time to make some new friends. In Chapter 7 we will talk about friendships and how to make new friends because, girl, every woman needs another woman she can have fun with from time to time, who understands her and she can share with sometimes. Otherwise who are we going to share period jokes or frustrations with and they totally get it? Or when our bra size is not ever on sale? Or when pregnancy cravings are trying to embarrass us? Or when we want to plan a surprise party for our husband? Or when we're losing our home-training because of work? Or we want our husband to plan a surprise party for us and we need someone to suggest it to him? I know you're married, girl, but once in a while you're *gonna* want to talk to another woman and it's perfectly okay.

Guess what, no matter how golden our friends are, it is still perfectly okay to go to the beach or go for ice-cream alone once in a while. The feeling is so peaceful and in those moments of aloneness, you sometimes get to hear your own heartbeat and remember who you really are. Away from all family and friends, yet secure in your own light and right. Once in a while, take yourself out and give yourself a nice treat. And if you're single, you stand a better chance of meeting someone of the opposite sex alone than with company. Oh, and how powerful it is to be caught having a good time by yourself. It speaks volumes of how enjoyable your company must be that you are willing to enjoy it all alone.

Sometimes I go to the cinema on a Monday morning when I figure everyone else would be at work, and I just sit in front of the big screen all alone enjoying the movie, I love to hear the sound of my laughter echo through the walls and the beautiful chill I feel from just being alone, aware and totally happy. My me-time is some of the best times of my life. Sometimes I go dancing with my husband and sometimes I go dancing with my girlfriends, but no matter who I go out with, I make sure that I am having the time of my life. Nothing less would suffice, only the highest possible good time is fit for a baby girl like you and I.

Parties and Love Feasts

One way to have fun in a group without bearing all the cost is to split the bills or simply do a BYOB (bring your own bottle), or potluck. That way, everybody brings something to the hangout or party and everybody enjoys. A love feast can be a great bonding experience for the entire family and everybody gets to have fun. Some people enjoy hosting while others do not, so we can take advantage of family birthdays, and anniversaries to plan a fun party. We don't even need an excuse to party, sometimes we should just invite friends over just because, FRIENDSHIP!

Back in the university, I had a great time cooking and hosting friends from school and church after the end of exams every semester, we had such a good time telling stories and simply enjoying each other's company all day long. If it is your cup of tea, then go ahead and plan a family picnic or outing with friends and everybody gets to chip in one way or another.

Get a Massage

Nothing spells being pampered quite like a gentle massage.

In massage therapy, a trained, certified massage therapist manipulates the soft tissues of your body — muscle, connective tissue, tendons, ligaments and skin. There are different levels of pressure and movements employed for different types of massages. So, if it is your first time, please ask questions and don't be shy to ask for a recommendation with your personal history in mind. It was one of my girlfriends who first took me to get a massage at the spa and, boy, I haven't stopped going ever since.

Because massage is generally considered a part of integrative medicine, it works wonders in relieving the body of stress and triggering physiological changes in our body through the relaxation response. Our body yearns for touch; it is a deep-seated desire in every human to be touched and in a loving way. So whether we have a partner that is willing to cover us in essential oils and give us a nice massage or we find our way to a spa or massage parlor, we can try to make massages a constant part of our life. A massage can make one soft to the touch and very relaxed and is great for improved sleep and digestion.

Depending on what our body needs per time, we can always choose from a wide variety of massage options, commonly referred to as modalities. There are so many of them and I've only ever experienced a handful. Here are some of the most popular and what they entail.

1. Swedish Massage: This is a traditional massage and typically involves some kneading, stroking, and friction using massage oils to loosen muscular tension and increase blood circulation. You are expected to take off your clothes and are free to request a masseuse of your gender. Duration is usually about 35 to 60 minutes but may vary depending on the spa or massage parlor.

2. Craniosacral Therapy: If you are still unsure about removing your clothes for a total stranger to give you a massage, then you may consider the Craniosacral therapy. Same light touch, same restorative effect, but completely non-invasive and fully clothed. You may sit or lie down for this.

3. Pregnancy Massage: If you have ever been pregnant, then you may have experienced the silly aches that come with it. In some women it is quite mild but in other women, it is severe. Whichever part of the spectrum we belong, a nice pregnancy massage can help us feel better and additionally help regulate our hormones, improve sleep and reduce swelling and pains in the back and joints. Pregnancy is a sensitive time so be sure that only a certified therapist whose specialty is prenatal massage attends to you if you ever sign up for a pregnancy massage. And feel free to ask a thousand questions till you are comfortable and confident with the procedure.

4. Aromatherapy Massage: Imagine being a Queen in ancient Egypt and enjoying the best of back rubs and full body massages with the most exquisite essential oils while lounging lazily and daydreaming about your good life. Now wake up. That's the best way I can describe an aromatherapy massage as it infuses essential oils like peppermint, lavender, cypress, sandalwood Peppermint, tea tree etc. Jasmine helps with libido, while Chamomile is used to improve mood and relaxation, so depending on your needs, you can explain to your massage therapist and see which essential oils they have available and what the effects are for you. Remember; your body, your preferences. Ask the right questions before your Aromatherapy massage and you're likely to get the best possible treatment.

5. Deep Tissue Massage: This is one massage that I would only suggest to someone who really needs a deep tissue work, perhaps to correct issues relating to posture, or severe muscle pain. It can be quite painful as the masseuse would typically use knuckles, hands, and elbows to really work the kinks out of the body. If you are unwell or have inflamed joints, then this may not be the massage for you as you don't want to worsen issues. The first and only time I got a deep tissue massage, I had to follow up with more subtle relaxation massages to balance out the effect. Nevertheless, it can be an effective type of massage if you need an intense work. Speak with a professional first to be sure you are ready for this.

6. Hot Stone Massage: If you enjoy warm baths and saunas, then you may be in for a treat with a hot stone massage. Hours after a hot stone massage I would usually still feel the heat on my back seeping slowly into my skin. The masseuse would place hot stones on your body, alternating between her hands and the stones while giving you a massage. It is quite a comforting feeling especially when paired with the other massage modalities. The heat makes for a great after-effect and helps to loosen tension in your body and the reward is a good night sleep.

There are so many other modalities of massages and whenever you're ready, you'll be sure pleased with the calming effects of a good massage on your body and mind.

Vacations

A vacation is one sure way to explore the world and meet new people. Whether alone, with family or friends, vacations are always worth the time and effort that go into planning them. How often we go on vacation depends on a variety of factors including how much funds we have available and how much time we are able to steal away in a year. For some people, vacationing has become a way of life and they save both money and time towards this fun experience all year round. I know some people who travel somewhere every month, don't ask me how they manage the balance. I reckon that they've chosen to prioritize adventure and it is working for them.

If you love to explore different cultures and food, then choose to go on destination vacations abroad or simply go somewhere fun around your city, but whichever you choose, a vacation is a sure good way to have fun. Exciting and completely refreshing, consider if you love beaches or hillsides when choosing a vacation destination. Some places are popular for mountain-climbing while others are popular for their nature parks and wildlife, and some others are popular for high-rise shopping malls. There are many fun activities to explore on a vacation like a visit to the animal zoo, a botanical garden, an aquarium, a museum, landmark centres in that city, golf, ziplining, ice skating and the list goes on and on and on. If you have children, then for sure, you are giving them memories to cherish for a lifetime. So be sure to include your man and your children on some vacation time for a great family bonding experience.

Where we go, what we wear, and what we do on vacation should be decided primarily by what we love so let's make it fun, and go with the people we love and care about. And come home refreshed and ready to take on new horizons. Thankfully, there are lots of travel agencies and planning outfits that can help us decide the best vacation spots round the year, so a little research will reveal the ones in our vicinity, so we can use their services if we don't want to plan our trips by ourselves. But make up your mind that pampering yourself and going on vacations is reserved specifically for you. Spread your wings and fly, baby!.

Retreats and Resorts

Sometimes all we need to get that big idea for our business or big break is a retreat. We can take some time off and go to a quiet place alone or in a group with our team and unplug from the busy buzz of everyday life. If we can, it may be a nice touch to keep cell phones and digital devices away, even if just for a few hours in the day and take a pen and paper along. Retreats are very great for unwinding and offer a much bigger emotional and mental reward. When we make it a spiritual retreat, the rewards can be far more profound for our all round wellness.

On a retreat, we want to pay attention to what we eat and what we listen to or watch. A total purging of the very things that harass our daily life can prove effective for a renewed version of ourselves. So next time we go on a retreat, we should try to be deliberate about what we focus our energy on and watch how our creative juices flow.

Budgets

In chapter 8, we talk about budgets and how to plan our finances to afford the lifestyle we desire and deserve. When we are deliberate about our income, savings and investment, we will have enough money to fund our relaxation as often as we desire. Once we have a shift in our mindset and first accept that the good life is for us, then funding it becomes an easier matter. Start where you are, there is so much fun calling out to you from all around your immediate environment. Start there and move up the ladder, girlfriend.

*Then Jesus said, "Come to me, all of
you who are weary and carry heavy
burdens, and I will give you rest.*
- Matthew 11:28

CHAPTER 7
LOVE AND RELATIONSHIPS

Buogo had picked out the most beautiful lilies from the flower shop, and as she headed over to Pam's house, she made one quick stop at Mickey's bar and grill to get the juiciest steaks that Pam would absolutely love.

It had been a month now since Pam had returned from the hospital. They had all been so scared for her. The doctors had discovered her blood count was low and had placed her on some simple diet and medication to improve her health. Apparently, she lost a lot of blood during the delivery of the twins and had continued life normally without taking a much needed break. And even now, in classic Pam style, she had gone straight back to work after she returned from the hospital. It took her husband threatening to involve her parents to get her to finally obey the Doctor's orders and go home. Now they were making her take a mandatory two weeks break from work. She had dismissed the idea of seeing a therapist to discuss what she had experienced and chose instead to talk to Buogo. And in classic Buogo style, she had put in for an unpaid leave from work to go and take care of her *bestie*.

Providence must be smiling at them, because Adjoa had invited them on a ladies vacation trip to her home city of Accra. When they protested the expenses, she assured them they would be her guests as she had an exquisite villa home in Accra. They had gotten pretty close, Adjoa and Buogo, and she found out some intriguing details about this former model who had struggled with an eating disorder after a particularly painful separation from her husband. Providence was definitely smiling at them all, because her estranged husband was now eager for a reunion and had even flown in twice to visit her in her Lagos home. Buogo was determined to make this the most fun ladies' vacation for herself and her girlfriends. And once she hinted to Chrissy and Lara, her closest colleagues at work, that she was going on a sponsored vacation, they were both eager to get away and have a good time.

She smiled as she waited patiently in the Lagos traffic, nodding to the voice of her latest crush on radio. His name was Teddy, and she daydreamed that he was a real life Teddy that she could snuggle close to every night. She had checked him out on Instagram and he was all that, huge enough for her to fit perfectly in his embrace and with a glowing chocolate skin. The only thing was that he seemed to have a squint eye and she didn't know what to make of that. She had sent him a direct message to say that she enjoyed his shows and could they grab a drink sometime. The message had been left unread for way too long and she wondered if he ever saw it. She shook her head to push the thoughts away as a careless bike rider swerved into her lane, almost knocking off her side mirror. Deep breath, deep breath, she reminded herself of her Yoga instructors popular phrase. She felt the anger die away almost as quickly as it rose in her as she took deep soulful breaths and continued on her journey.

She had every reason to be thankful, friends who she could count on to drop their work and come away with her and friends who could count on her to be there for them. She was rich in the things that mattered to her. She stayed a few minutes longer in the car, just to hear Teddy sign off in his usual baritone, 'Till I come your way next time, think of me as I think of you, your Teddy'.

She melted as the sound of the old school classic; *When a Woman Loves* filled her automobile. She was sure going to miss Teddy on this trip. As she grabbed the flowers and pack of juicy steaks to head upstairs, she smiled to think what fun adventure lay before the five of them for the next one week. She had absolutely no idea what they were in for.

Just as she locked her car door, a message came in her DM. It was Teddy.

****

It would seem that the more technologically advanced we get as a people, the more socially impeded we tend to become. While we acknowledge that the top can be a lonely place, yet it must not necessarily be so. 'The higher you go, the lonelier it becomes', should not be a phrase that we welcome and celebrate. TI am all for organic social networks and real life experiences with other humans because I believe that as humans, we never outgrow a need for physical human connections. We cannot continue to hide behind our phones and act surprised when we hear that someone committed suicide. Why didn't they talk to someone? We ask. Or why didn't they reach out for help? But all around us are people whose eyes are filled with pain and grief and who are hungry for our leftovers. If we don't take a moment to look up from our mobile phones, and laptops and spare them one look, we may never see the things they are too afraid to say. Their eyes tell a deep story but we need to take a break from our own lives and look at the next person and offer a smile or a gentle hand squeeze to reassure them of the value of life.

As women, we have to be deliberate about cultivating relationships, especially, if we hope to go far in our personal lives, careers and as home makers. So often, we hear the phrase, *if you want to go fast, go alone, but if you want to go far, go with someone.* Friendship and relationships are essential to a woman's mental health and this is because woman is a social being. And every time I hear that 'your network is your net worth', I smile in agreement. That is why I love HASHTAGS that celebrate women supporting women and I have been eagerly at the forefront of impactful women summits and conferences, as much as possible, over the years.

I am deliberate about building and maintaining relationships, so much that my only resolution in 2020 was to be a better friend, and so I called my close friends and made a new pledge of commitment and began to go out of my way to show up for them, even more than ever before. The effects on my friends and on me are so beautiful and so numerous that they probably deserve an entire book on to it. From shared vacations and hangouts, to renewed family connections, spiritual awakenings, and mind blowing business opportunities, it is a decision that brings me wide smiles anytime I remember.

Let us continue to shake off the false crippling notion that women do not genuinely love each other, because I have learnt from personal experience as well as history that women can be each other's best allies and partners.

In 2021, I am taking a step further to concentrate on my family relationships, focusing mostly on my two nuclear families made up of my birth parents and siblings and my husband and daughter. I believe that relationships are foundational and everything rises and falls on quality organic relationships and friendships.

Doors have opened to me in places that only solid relationships have the key, and this is what social networking is all about.

I will always be an advocate of building wholesome human relationships across different cadres of life. It may be the one hope we have of restoring our humanity and navigating life in one piece and peace.

Before we dismiss the possibilities of building truly mutually beneficial authentic relationships in this day and age, let us first open our mind as we explore what some relationship blockers and impediments can be and how to effectively navigate them to enjoy what may very well be, the glue to living a holistic life. For an adult, there are various relationships necessary for a balanced life. We will find that in our day-to-day living, we experience interactions that cut across one or more of the following relationships discussed in this chapter. So let us talk love and relationships, shall we.

7.1 FAMILY RELATIONSHIPS

As far back as primary school, we had been taught that family is the smallest unit of society, consisting of father, mother and children. It wasn't until much later in life that I would come to realize just how fundamental the family unit is in the grand scheme of society's existence. It is interesting how everything rises and falls on the family system, whether they be vices or virtues, strengths or weaknesses, we are all a reflection of our basic nature and nurture. So, when anything happens in society, we often look back to the family and wonder, whose daughter is she? Where does she come from? Does she even have home training? Her parents must be so proud, they did a good job raising her. Whether a woman is judged as good or bad, society often holds the family responsible for how we turn out. To a great extent, I am inclined to agree with the rest of society. Even modern science dictates that genes are passed down from parents to their children, which gives credence to the fact that our nature is gotten mostly from our family, and sociology/psychology suggests that our nurture is the construct of our family. Therefore it stands to reason that the pursuit of holistic living for a woman must make room to accommodate relationships that exist within the family, whether she perceives her family to be good or bad, and whether these relationships have negative or positive effects. If we are in good terms with our family or if we are estranged, we are relating with them somewhat. The dynamics of that relationship however, can go a long way to influence our understanding of who we are. Recall that earlier in this book, we discussed perceptions so it is my hope that we can look beyond the seeming imperfections of our families, steering away from any landmines therein with a laser focus goal in mind, to mine the gold existing within this brave entity called FAMILY.

To look ahead, let us first look back.

FAMILY LANDMINES

There are a great many reasons why a woman may not desire or even pursue a healthy relationship with her father, mother or siblings. Many of these reasons surround issues of pain, lack, anger, jealousy and betrayal that were mostly experienced in the formative years while growing up. From teenage hood, a woman's sense of freedom is developed and if she judges her family to be hostile, unloving, or economically incapable of taking care of any of her needs, rebellion can usually be the first recourse especially in instances where the parents present a disunited front. Love is a great shield for many of us, so whether we come from a poor or rich family, as long as there is evident love between mother and father and towards the children, the family system is at equilibrium and the children grow up with a desire to stay in touch. This may be the reason why some of the worst hit children when it comes to the issue of identity crisis and self esteem issues, are children from broken homes where the parents are divorced, separated, or simply have some form of marriage crisis like domestic violence and other forms of abuse.

If one grew up in a dysfunctional family, chances are that she would not have a great desire to stay in touch with people who only remind her of a bitter past, a past that she works hard each day to escape, erase or rewrite. But I fear that we may never truly be able to completely run from our past. My heart goes out to every woman who endured any form of abuse in the family growing up. It creates such a big hole in one's heart that she may spend the rest of her life trying to fill it, sometimes with little or no success, from mindless love relationships to tolerating abuse in the workplace and friendships. A woman may go on from person to person, and from place to place, seeking for the love that she doesn't get from her family.

Dealing with a traumatic childhood can be a massive roadblock towards attaining full discovery and personal freedom. But again, we cannot hide from our past, no matter how hard we try. The blood coursing through our veins is proof of our eternal ties to a family unit, and whether we hate them or love them, we simply cannot cut them away from our existence. It is hard to embrace family relationships when the dynamics of that relationship are laced with so many social landmines like sexual abuse, verbal abuse, gross neglect, physical abuse, sibling rivalry, sibling strife and abuse, preferential treatments, all forms of lovelessness and even absolute abandonment. However, I have come to find that there is often a small room present in our hearts from where forgiveness can grow and a healthy family relationship can begin to thrive, even after years of estrangement or bitterness. And if there is even the smallest possibility that we open our heart to feel all the pain as raw and as violent as it may seem, and begin to nurture a desire for healing and a renewal of the family relationship, I am persuaded by personal experiences and the testimonies of others before us, that healing is possible. Restoring a relationship with our family may not be an instant thing, but if you are open to go on this journey, I am here to hold your hands as we explore ways to renew relationships with the very first members of our society.

Growing Up

The first friendships

Issues of sibling rivalry exist largely because of our human differences, which are a primary function of our nature and nurture. There is a popular saying amongst the Igbo people to whom I belong which goes, *ofu nne na-amu, mana oburo ofu chi na-eke*, this loosely translates as, motherhood may be common, but identity is individual. Growing up, my siblings and I had some rough moments where we fought and even refused to allow one person or the other go out with one or more of us. As the 4th in a family of 5, I was mostly withdrawn, thinking one thing and doing yet another. It was easy to feel like a part of a bigger picture and subtly overlook the uniqueness of my own individuality. So often times, I would sulk because one of my siblings was mean to me, never quite understanding why. When I got much older, I realized that quarrels, fights and arguments were popular amongst siblings in many different homes. It wasn't only happening in my family like I had assumed.

On different levels and for different reasons, siblings do not always agree with each other. I did not like it then and I still do not like it now. But one thing has changed for me and helped me relate much better with my own siblings than I did years before, and that is that I have come to a place where I see that every fight or quarrel was a misunderstanding stemming primarily from our individual differences. Yes, we are siblings, but at each time we are manifesting the differences present in our basic nature. There is a reason one sibling will keep the group's secret and the other one will sell the rest of the siblings out. It may have nothing to do with wickedness or stupidity but may simply be a function of their very own personal make up. They may simply be trying to protect themselves or court the love and attention of perhaps a distracted parent. Firstborns have their characteristic tendencies as do middle children and lastborns, only daughters and only sons as well. Again, consider that even outside of your own family group, there is all manner of disagreements amongst members of the same playgroup, church, and even school. Foolishness is very popular amongst children, and so must be regarded as such. We were young, and we didn't know better, so somehow we hurt the people that we truly loved most, even without realizing the damage we were doing. And today, these people crawl into their shells and we wonder why our siblings don't just call or visit us.

We may remember playing fun games with them growing up but all they remember is being compared to us in the Sciences and being made to look like a fool in the family. And while we remember being the worst cook in the family, they may remember us bullying them out of their own lunch money. Sometimes, they remember how we may have preferred our friends over them, and openly mocked them before their playmates for bedwetting or some other nonsensical issue. While these may seem nonsensical to us, it may have formed a pain in their heart that causes them to look down and walk only on the side of the room, never ever feeling enough. So you see, our sister or brother doesn't really miss our calls because they were busy at work, and neither did they actually forget to visit on our birthday, they probably just can't stand us because they are holding on to the past hurt and humiliations that they hold us responsible for. And this weighs them down, consciously or subconsciously, and they carry it with them everywhere, but we don't see it because we are different from them, we are not as emotional as they are, and we do not remember things as vividly as they do. Or maybe we are fortunate to be so positive that we do not dwell on past hurts or we are simply wise enough to understand that these were all childish gimmicks.

> **Non-forgiveness and bitterness can rub people of so much joy and it is quite a shame how things that happened decades ago can continue to weigh someone down even until today.**

But in reality they do, and as much as we may not like or agree with the reasons they do, siblings grow distant and sometimes forget one another.

Do you have a good relationship with your siblings? Or has past hurts caused you to forget the many good times that you shared together?

Try to put yourself in the shoes of your siblings, what would you have done differently? It is possible that if you had their genetic makeup and lived with their everyday fears and pain, you may have treated people the same way they did. It is also possible that you may not have. But the point I'd like us to consider is that humans make mistakes, because we are imperfect and we are different from each other. Our genetic make-up and personal struggles, partner with our perceptions, biases, convictions and nurture to make us who we are.

Tim LaHaye in Why You Act The Way You Do outlined 4 basic temperament types; Melancholy, Sanguine, Choleric and Phlegmatic. He went further to propose 16 different blends of these temperament and argued that we all fall into at least one of these different blends. An understanding of our human strengths and weaknesses help us to act better. When he released another book on temperaments, Spirit-Controlled Temperament, he went ahead to suggest that as humans, we can go beyond simply understanding why we act the way we do, to actually seek to use this knowledge of our basic strengths and weakness, as a force for personal change, instead of an excuse to dismiss our shortcomings. Simply, when we know what our weaknesses are, we can work to strengthen them and even smell temptations from miles away and when we know our strengths, we can be deliberate about preserving them and seeking opportunities to amplify and use them for personal and greater good. Minimizing our weaknesses and maximizing our strengths is a discipline every one of us must pursue, but it begins with an understanding of self. Why do we act the way we do?

When our siblings hurt us, realize it, and apologize, it is our duty to forgive them and relate with them in a way that is mutually beneficial, being careful not to be repeatedly drawn into any toxicity that is in their own nature. When we hurt our siblings and realize it, we must also apologize and hope that they forgive us and the relationship is restored. But when we have hurt our siblings in the past or they have hurt us, and neither of us realize the wrong we have done, it is a matter of understanding. Simply, we do not understand our own self or we do not understand the offended person so we are not even aware that a wrong has been committed and we do not realize there is a need to apologize and forgive. You are the one reading this so you are presented with an opportunity to begin a process of reconciliation and restoration. It is up to you to ask yourself if you are alright with carrying the burden of sibling rivalry and allowing it affect your relationship with your first friends and blood siblings, and if it is worth it that after all these years, you are still unable to genuinely build a wholesome relationship with your siblings. If your answer is NO, then perhaps it is time to make amends, irrespective of who the offender is. If you have been hurt, then reach out and let them know they hurt you, if you suspect that you are the one that hurt them which is why they do not enjoy your company, then perhaps reach out and apologize.

Josh Mcdowell's Handbook on counseling youth, co-authored by Josh Mcdowell and Bob Hostetler suggest that the effects of sibling abuse, in severe cases can carry on into adulthood and produce the same results as any form of abuse, including feelings of guilt, mistrust, aggression, deficient social skills, insecurity and poor self esteem.

It is time to break away from every negativity that may have been presented in our life by sibling rivalry and rebuild our relationship with our siblings. There is a healing that comes when we are at peace with our family, and the effects of that healing can have a ripple effect that even shows in other aspects of our life and in our relationship with other people. Embrace a relationship with your siblings and hopefully it turns your life around.

If one is already a mother with young children, she must also be vigilant and do her best to discourage sibling rivalry, strife and abuse amongst her children, to avoid its future negative effects. Perhaps the words of Adele Faber and Elaine Mazlish, co-authors of Siblings Without Rivalry, will help us. They suggest that intellectually, sibling rivalry may not be hard to understand but, emotionally, many of us have difficulty accepting young people's hostile feeling towards each other. Perhaps we might better understand those feelings if we put ourselves in their place.

Personally, I suggest that whether we experienced such rivalry or sibling abuse in our childhood or not, it is important to watch out for them in our children to avoid it's negative impacts in our children's lives later on. We should discourage name-calling, physical fights, and avoid critical comparison of one child to the other. Additionally, let us do our best to learn the distinct personalities of each of our children so we can help them harness their strengths and improve on their weaknesses, celebrating each person's individuality and victories rather than judging all of them by the same yardstick. One child may be good at Physics while another child may be good at drawing and yet another good at baking, we should do our best to celebrate each one as publicly as the other.

There is a second saying almost as popular as the first one, amongst the Igbos, concerning sibling relationships, they say, *iwe nwanne adighi eru na okpukpu*. Which roughly means that a sibling's wrong is easier to forgive. So open your heart and do your best to forgive, first for your own healing and ultimately so you can enjoy the rewards of a renewed relationship with your siblings.

Reconnecting with Your Roots

As important as a good relationship with our siblings is, I am persuaded that it is even more important to have a good relationship with our parents. As a woman, one's relationship with her mother may help her understand parts of herself she struggles with. When you finally become a mother, she may help you understand the beautiful journey you're set to embark on.

The issue of relationship with parents can be quite sensitive, especially because there's a great age gap between us as children and our parents. This generational gap can be a barrier but it can also hold some answers to the questions of why our parents raised us the way they did. Consider that our parents grew up in very different times than we did.

So maybe we can ask ourselves, what did our parents learn about raising children from their own parents? What was life like for them as children and young parents? How did the dynamics of their marriage influence the way they raised us? Do they have any regrets about how they raised us? Are they proud of how we turned out? How were they raised? What were their own core values and how did it influence their parenting style? What knowledge and materials on parenting were available to them when they raised us?

If we can honestly answer these questions for ourselves, I believe that we may begin to understand that our parents may have done the best they could, given who they were, what they knew and what they had. If we are truly unable to answer those questions then we have to genuinely desire to find out the answers and to even ask ourselves if we ever truly cared enough to find out what life for our parents has been. Do they have dreams? What did they have to give up for our sake? Who hurt them in their past? Are they living a happy life? Did they even realize the full responsibilities of parenthood before having children?

Seek to know the answer to these questions, whether you think your parents raised you well or not. The answer to these questions may not only help you understand your parents and what influenced how they raised you and your siblings but will perhaps help you to consciously begin to seek a better understanding of your own self in a bid to be a better parent.

It wasn't until I had my daughter that I began to really understand what my parents may have experienced in raising me and my four siblings. Every day, I face my own battles both within me and outside and whether I win or lose, I have to do my best to be a good mother to November. And guess what, whether she grows up to judge my best efforts to be enough or not, I will know that I always did my best as her parent with what I know, what I have, and given who I am. One of the best things I can do for her is to pursue a stable relationship with her father who is my husband and in so doing raise her in the most stable home filled with all the love and security that money cannot buy. Everything else is secondary, because I believe that love and the security it brings is the greatest need of a child.

If for different reasons our parents did not provide us with that love, perhaps because they simply were distracted by the cares of life or the issues in their own marriage or they did not have it in themselves to give or maybe they weren't interested enough to do so or they did not understand how to give us the love we needed in the way and at the time we needed it, then that is a sad tragedy. I am sincerely sorry that you had to go through all that you may have gone through. It would be understandable that you do not desire a relationship with them, the very people who were tasked with the responsibilities of loving and protecting you from all forms of emotional, sexual and physical abuse as well as providing the basic things you needed to feel loved, protected and cared for in such a vulnerable season of your life when you needed them most.

Issues of identity and self esteem stem primarily from parental neglect and abuse, and even though we may not realize it or even admit it, we were faced with a lot of abuse from a lot of parents who didn't know better growing up. The evidence is in the society we have today, rife with adults who perpetuate unthinkable vices and all forms of greed and corruption of power. We have bitter people leading us, angry men and women in our markets, teachers who vengefully punish children in the guise of discipline, guardians that batter house helps, fake drugs by heartless individuals, lovers who cheat on and maim their spouses, as well as men and women who take advantage of the young girls and boys that call them professor and boss.

> **The men and women in our society today reflect the families we come from. It is a vicious cycle, people who are hurt end up hurting others.**

But we are not helpless in this situation. If we must reclaim our society and transform our own lives as women, then we have to be deliberate about pursuing a better understanding of (and relationship with) our parents before us, irrespective of our perception of their parenting. The hope that we have of raising better children is building a relationship with our own parents, in order to understand them and see why they did what they did, and hopefully learn from their successes and mistakes. If we do not restore the relationships with our parents, then even with our good intentions, we may end up repeating the same mistakes we feel they made or worse in our children when we become parents because we will lack understanding.

> **To stop the cycle of hurt and abuse, we must forgive our own parents and make peace with our past, and simply stop running from our own shadow.**

So pursuing healing in our relationship with our parents, is firstly a matter of healing ourselves from the hurt and effects of the rejection we faced growing up and secondly, enjoying a closer bond with the people who form our foundation and identity, as well as a sure way to ensure that we do right by our own children.

Now, whether we believe our parents did right by us or not, we may need to consider that they truly did the best they could and whether they admit it or not, they may also struggle to sleep at night over the areas they have now realized that they failed us. Forgive them, even if they do not ask for forgiveness, and let a more meaningful relationship between you be restored, it is one of the best gifts one can give to the people who gave her life. When we are at peace with our parents and are happy with each other and enjoy a wholesome relationship, we will find that there is a renewal of our own sense of self and we will hurt way less. Let us do it for love, for our own selves, our parents and for our own children. Let us do it while our parents are still alive so that they too may heal and find peace in a loving relationship with their own child.

7.2 FRIENDSHIP/PLATONIC RELATIONSHIPS

I had an interesting conversation with renowned author, Chimamanda Ngozi Adichie, during an interview sometime in 2018. I had met her beloved mother at the salon while in the University of Nigeria, and she had spoken with so much pride about her daughter Chimamanda who at the time had just released her book, Americanah. Our conversation at the salon was sparked by our hairs which were virgin African hairs and was a common feature in the book Americanah and which we both seemed to flaunt with pride. It was on this chance encounter that I decided that Chimamanda, who I hadn't yet met, must be a lovely woman whose insights I may enjoy like I had enjoyed her mother's. So when I met Chimamanda a few years after this encounter with her mum, it was easier to go from just a formal interview to a more casual and relaxed conversation about culture, identity and being woman. She had given a heartwarming speech at the Face of Okija Cultural Festival in her home state of Anambra and so much of our interview was expected to be around that and perhaps the issue of feminism. However, we took a friendly drift and I asked her a question that seemed to take her aback a bit but then she smiled, and confessed she hadn't considered my question before and she went on to give an honest yet profound response.

I had asked her which endangered Igbo culture she would preserve if she had the power to do so for her daughter and other young girls to enjoy. And she told of Oyi-Uto, a culture practiced amongst her people that allowed a young girl to be identified with a male friend with whom she has only platonic friendship and nothing romantic. In this culture, the young girl and her oyiuto will typically go places like the stream together, play together and generally be spotted together. There were no speculations of immorality as in present times, and within the protection of this cultural practice, the young girl learns how to relate with the opposite sex without any negative public scrutiny, or the pressure presented by an insinuation of romantic interests and in all innocence and purity of heart. In this culture, they were just a boy and a girl who enjoyed each other's company and were allowed to simply be platonic friends.

I smiled to think of such a culture, and then we compared it to the predominant culture of judgment and suspicion that surrounds many pursuits of platonic friendships today. As young girls, we are often taught that teenage girls and boys cannot be friends and so when adulthood meets us, we do not even possess much understanding of the rudiments of dating, and courtship. How then are we expected to magically bring a man home when we are judged ready to marry at 23, after being sworn off male friends at 16? Most of our parents and guardians are quite funny in this respect, and I too, like Chimamanda, wish that the culture of Oyiuto, where a boy and girl can be friends with no strings attached and in all innocence can be resuscitated.

As women, If we have no experience or practice with making friends with young boys or even other girls at a younger age, chances are that we may find it a bit awkward to do so as adults either when we're ready to start dating and get married or even just to pursue platonic friendships for social reasons. Let us look at some ways that we can make friends at any age and stage of life, because we're never too old for friendship.

How to Make Friends

I like to think that making and keeping wholesome friendships is primarily a function of two things, the first is, being friendly and the second is, understanding how to service our friendships.

The easiest way we can make a new friend is simply to present ourselves as a friend. So if one wants to make a friend, then she needs to go places where she will actually meet other humans and be nice to somebody. Places like the gym, cinema, church, beach, dance club and salon are all great choices if one is looking to meet people who are not in a hurry to leave. So let's just say you sight someone who you consider would make for a goof friend. My advice would be to simply approach, introduce yourself and be sure to give the other person a chance to talk about themselves if they will. Most people love to talk about their passion and interests so take a genuine interest when you ask someone to tell you about themselves, and don't shut them up mid sentence. A simple conversation starter can be, I love your hairstyle, it really suits you or your outfit is nice, the color goes well with your skin tone. Then you can go on to ask them any questions relevant to the event of the day. This typically applies to both male and female friends and if we do this long enough, we are sure to have a few friends who we can enjoy simple fun activities and conversations with. Even if the first person you try to be friends with doesn't give off friendly vibes, feel free to move on to other persons who catch your interest. Anybody can be our friend if we are genuinely interested in them. And we are not desperate if we go out of our way to make a new friend, not every friendship is automatic, and some of the best friendships happen when people go out of their way to court the attention of someone they like and suspect they may enjoy their company. If anything, we are actually smart enough and respect ourselves if we are careful to observe people and reach out to those who we think may be a good fit, instead of just waiting around and settling for anyone chance brings our way. It is perfectly okay to select our friends.

One day, one of my oldest friends who I had attended primary and secondary school as well as university with came to visit me at the radio station where I worked as a Presenter and Producer at the time. After an enjoyable conversation, he mentioned that he has a friend whose friendship he thinks I would enjoy. The lady was someone we had attended secondary school and university with but somehow she and I were never quite friends in all that time. He said we both seemed to share the same value system and enjoy similar activities, so he encouraged me to reach out to her. Just as he had suspected, we hit it off so well that a few years later, she was beside me on my wedding day as one of my bridesmaids. We continue to enjoy a beautiful friendship that has involved us sharing good times, hangouts, dreams and even more friends. We have gone beyond social benefits to support each other in our careers and help each other spot and take up strategic opportunities. And it all began with a friendly suggestion.

Friendship is so beautiful and really vital to a woman's life, because a good friend is a great asset any day, any time. Even in marriage, we will still need friends for a ladies night out and occasional brunch. If you've ever gone to karaoke with a group of your girlfriends and simply sang your hearts out with them hyping you on even when everyone knows you're singing off-key, then you'll know that girlfriends are a must have for a modern woman.

Servicing Friendships

To find a friend is one thing, and to keep your friendship alive is an entirely different thing. There is a difference between having an acquaintance and having a friend. If we say that someone is our friend then we should hold each other accountable to the requirements of friendship. We should do our best to be there for one another as much as possible in the good times and bad times and to support each other on our life's journey. Celebrate the small wins of our friends and lend a helping hand whenever we can. Hype each other and build each other up and be committed to our mutual growth and happiness in all areas of our lives.

If we can remember the birthdays and important events in the life of a friend, then we should show up for them in a way that shows we love and care for them. A thoughtful gift however small can go a long way to show we care.

Having said this, let us be sure that our friendship is not one-sided, and our loyalty and dedication is reciprocated when the tables are turned.

Do not hesitate to walk away from any friendship that is toxic and seems to be one-sided where you are the one always giving and always making sacrifices. Friendship should be mutually beneficial and enjoyable, so any friend that keeps making you feel terrible about yourself or always has excuses why they can't be there for you when you really need them or makes a habit of betraying you should not be accommodated beyond reason. Do not give toxic friends any room in your life. We do not choose our parents and siblings but we choose who our friends can be. Thankfully, friendship is not by blood, it is a choice and one can always walk away at any point in time. There are many more friends out there who will love you and treat you like the queen you are, and these are the men and women you should pursue friendship with.

7.3 ROMANTIC RELATIONSHIPS

Let's talk about love, baby. The subject of love and romance is probably the biggest theme of most movies, book, songs and all art forms. Everybody is talking about love. Meanwhile Eros love is only one form of love, and while there are so many others, this is the one most women concern ourselves with from early teenage years of Mills and Boons into the years beyond. A lot has been said about dating and courtship and marriage so I will do my best to shed a little light on an aspect of love that we rarely discuss. That aspect is, understanding one's own self in the love equation. So let's talk about why we love the way we love and how we can give and receive love better.

Love Yourself First

There are a few concepts that can help us as women to understand ourselves best and access the best possible love available. They include an understanding of the primary love languages, an appreciation of the difference between being alone and being lonely, mutual respect and the need for setting personal boundaries, expectations and privacy.

Alone But Never Lonely

To be alone is to be without company but to be lonely is to be sad because we do not have company. Often times, as women, we make the erroneous assumption that loneliness is a factor of being alone, and that a relationship is the ultimate cure to loneliness. How misleading an assumption this can be. History has shown time and time again, women who were truly miserable and lonely even in some of the seeming most beautiful relationships. Loneliness, like boredom, is more about the individual than it is about company. So, I like to think that every women should do her best to learn the art of being alone but not lonely before she enters a relationship so that she will not hang her happiness and joy on the neck of her companion.

> ***We need to come to a place where we are comfortable in our own company; otherwise we stand the risk of becoming a puppet in another person's story.***

We can seek ways to find happiness by ourselves because as well intentioned as a relationship can be, it very rarely ever cures the loneliness we think it will. Even when we marry, we may be shocked to find that if we don't have our own personal life, it is easy to assume that our spouse doesn't care for our happiness sometimes; meanwhile our happiness was never their responsibility in the first place. If we do what it takes to find happiness by ourselves, we may notice that relationships, whether dating, courtship or marriage, do not define our happiness.

> ***Companionship is great, but very rarely does it cure loneliness.***

If in doubt, ask the many women in relationships who feel miserable, even though they claim they have wonderful partners and they never quite seem to walk away perhaps because they were just as miserable when they were single. Again, consider that there is another group of women who seem to always overflow with happiness and a deep glow whether they are single, dating, engaged or married. I do not have all the answers but I am honest enough to admit that loneliness is not always curable by romantic relationships. It is a myth sold to women mostly by arts and drama over the years but many women have found it out to be a lie. If one desires to stop being lonely, then she should seek to find ways to stay happy and create opportunities for herself to experience true happiness. This is why we have discussed the different things in this book like the need for a meaningful work, exercise, rest and relaxation, as well as hobbies and now friendships and relationships. Let us not put the responsibility of our life's joy on a fellow human. It is too much of a responsibility to leave in the hands of another person, especially one who is not our maker and who doesn't know the innermost desires of our heart.

We know ourselves better than any man ever could, so let's act like it. The truth is that if we look into our heart long enough, we may find out the real reason for our loneliness. Then we can be honest enough with ourselves to deal with whatever it is that makes us so lonely and pushes us to sometimes seek companionship in the wrong places. When we have resolved the issue of loneliness in our own life, then we will be ready to enjoy wholesome relationships and be happy enough with our own company even when we're single. It is then that we are able to set boundaries, limits and enforce privacy in any relationship or friendship that is unhealthy or toxic to our well being, whether in our workplace, love-life, family or friendship. Sadly, many women continue to stay in abusive relationships because they do not take responsibility for their own happiness and the fear of being alone cripples them and forces them to stay trapped where they shouldn't be.

Until we find fulfillment and happiness within us, we may never really be strong enough to enforce any boundaries or limits in our relationships because of the fear of being left alone. There is absolutely nothing wrong with being alone, once we discover how to be alone and not lonely. This is the way for people to stop taking advantage of us, when they see that we are happy alone, they will know that they have two options, either they treat us right and continue to enjoy the awesomeness that we are or they risk losing us because they know we will walk away. People will treat us how we allow, so let us normalize being treated only as the queens we are.

Our past is past, and as we deal with any pain and trauma from the past, we will find the healing we need and be totally free to lead happy lives.

So find a job that you love, and devote your heart to it, take up a new hobby, join a gym, travel with friends, sign up for a new course, visit your parents, connect with your siblings, go on a vacation alone, create a playlist of your favorite songs to enjoy, create time for a spiritual retreat, or volunteer somewhere you love. **You Are Enough** even on your journey of self-discovery. It is okay to be alone, but whether you're alone or with company, try not to be lonely.

> *It is always better to be alone than to be in bad company, so be patient girlfriend, the right relationships will always come along.*

What is Your Love Language?

An understanding of how we express and receive love is necessary so that we do not waste our time and energy on things that do not really matter to us or our partner whenever we find ourselves in a romantic relationship. Gary Chapman in his book, The 5 Love Languages established that men and women receive and give love in five basic ways. They include Words of Affirmation, Acts of Service, Receiving Gifts, Quality Time, and Physical Touch. While they are all very important ways of expressing and receiving love, some women find that they feel loved if their partner does some things more than others. So one woman may feel loved when her man spends time taking a stroll with her and another woman may feel loved when her man buys her a nice dress. And one woman may feel loved when her man compliments her and another woman may feel loved when her own man holds her hands during a leisure outing. It all boils down to understanding what matters to you so you can point your lover in the right direction whenever he wants to show you some extra TLC (tender love and care). But in doing this, be careful not to exaggerate your appreciation of one love language at the unnecessary detriment of the other. Yes, you love gifts but do not present yourself in such a way that may suggest that once a man buys you gifts, he does not need to compliment you from time to time.

Marriage

I am no expert on marriage, having only been married a few years. So when it comes to the issue of marriage, as most other things, I suppose there is no *one size fits all*. There may be good marriages and bad marriages but what marriage we have most often begins way before we even get married, from the expectations we have for our marriage and the work we choose to do in ourselves to prepare ourselves for when the time comes. Accepting a marriage proposal may depend on what we think we deserve and what we think we're worth. It can be such a sensitive decision that I believe we should do with as much clarity as possible so that we marry someone we are happy to wake up next to for the rest of our lives.

I have hosted a lot of weddings over the past 10 years and can guess which couples may have a more wholesome marriage, if appearances are anything to go by. From the wedding day, a bridegroom and his bride already display subtle signs of what their future together may look like. Once, I had a couple who couldn't agree whether the DJ or the music band should play the song for their first dance and the bride burst into tears when the husband eventually insisted on having his own way, and another time, I had a couple who spent all their time on the dance floor dancing with each other lost in the sweetness of their own company on the dance floor.

Yet the real marriage is not the wedding day but everything after we say I Do, and sometimes what we see on the wedding day is not always what we get in the marriage. That is why I consider a woman blessed if she makes the decision of a life partner with the help of God.

Let us consider one aspect of marriage for the modern day woman who seeks all round enjoyment in her new home.

Sexual Intimacy in Marriage

A lot is said about sexual abstinence and purity before marriage, and so I think even much more needs to be said about sexual intimacy when a woman does get married. Right from childhood, through adolescence and adulthood, the woman is taught such little sex education. At home and in school, the subject of sex is approached with a great level of secrecy, almost as though it is a taboo subject. So, it should not come as a surprise when a women finds herself in marriage but does not even know the first thing about sex and has no idea who to ask the right questions about sex. I consider sex as one of the most beautiful experiences in marriage, which can be as enjoyable for the woman as it is for the man and I figure that if more women know more about sex, they would see it as an enjoyable practice to look forward to and enjoy in marriage, not just something to avoid when single and even in marriage.

We looked at some exercises that can help a woman build confidence and stamina in order to be a better sex partner and even achieve orgasms in chapter 5. Sex is not merely a task for a married woman to satisfy her husband or to give excuses and avoid or only for procreation, as often wrongly peddled. So let us consider some of the benefits a holistic sexual experience can bring for a woman especially one who understands the purpose of sex.

HEALING AND RESTORATION

Somebody sang a song about Sexual Healing and I thought it was just a song until I experienced it. Good sex can boost our immunity and help relief stress. Depending on the frequency and intensity, sex can be considered a form of aerobic exercise burning up to 200 calories per session. But this is not the type where we just lie back and zone off leaving all the work to our spouse. We have to get involved and practice some of the maneuvers that regular exercise prepares us for. And we already discussed how great exercise is for the body. If a woman has regular sex with her spouse, her body produces higher levels of estrogen, which can give the skin a more supple feel and even protect her from osteoporosis, and heart diseases. Even her husband isn't left out from the benefits. Heart attacks are less likely in couples who enjoy loving sexual intercourse with their own spouse, where there is no fear of being caught by anybody.

> **The body also releases endorphins during sex which help stimulate immune system cells that fight diseases.**

According to a study by sexologist and author, Beverly Whipple, professor emeritus at Rutgers University, an orgasm can make the pain tolerance threshold and pain detection threshold increase significantly, by up to 74.6 percent and 106.7 percent in a woman.

RELAXATION AND ENJOYMENT

This is the biggest we tend to focus on in everyday sex. Whether we have sex twice a day, twice a week or twice a month, it is sure a good way to relax and enjoy ourselves with our spouse. If we take a moment to forget about the troubles of life and calm any anxieties we experience whenever the subject of sex comes up, then we can focus, instead, on finding creative ways to enjoy sex. You and your spouse can try to give each other massages first or listen to good music or oil yourselves up lovingly or simply enjoy a warm cuddle before sex, all these will leave you feeling generally more relaxed and will add to the enjoyment in your sex life. I have heard about couples who set sex dates and just go about their day knowing there's a date coming up later that week and it's all about sex. We're married but that doesn't mean we have to become boring. We can always explore new places to have sex. If you and your partner are faithful to each other sexually, then expect that you may feel some type of high after intercourse, as studies suggest that in monogamous relationships, the semen packs some mood-altering hormones that can promote good mood and relaxation leaving one feeling fly. I can't say I fully understand how this works but I don't want to argue with science that I've actually also experienced.

Book a weekend getaway with your husband, and perhaps go to a hotel nearby just for a change of scenery once in a while. Excite each other and understand that you have everything it takes within you to reach an orgasm if you establish good communication between you and your spouse. Do not be too shy to tell him what you love and what you do not like. Oh, I used to be so shy but I am happy to be in a place where I can express myself freely and enjoy the benefits. As we drop all inhibitions and master our body through the exercises we discussed earlier, we are more likely to experience earth shattering or blissful orgasms, depending on our body's unique functions.

Listen, orgasms are good and all, but, have you ever cuddled under the duvet during rain just before you *do the do*? Perfection.

SLEEP INDUCING

Marriage is a beautiful thing, you can't tell me otherwise. I mean, how can we explain that we can lie with our spouse after a long and stressful day, and end up having all our stress melt away just by a simple act of lovemaking. We may not even need sleeping pills if we have an active sex life, as having an orgasm will naturally lead to a release of sleep-inducing hormones like Serotonin that will make us drowsy and probably send us straight to sleep. So, if you want to sleep like a baby, tap your husband and give him your secret signal to meet you in the bedroom. A full 8 hour long night of sleep may be your reward. Absolutely worth it for someone who enjoys a good night rest.

CREATIVITY

I will not dwell on this because I do not know for sure if this is just me. But I have found that I can be at my best creative self after a wonderful sex time with my husband. Perhaps this is a function of the hormones released during sex, or maybe it is more a function of the state of rest that my mind goes into after sex, but I am convinced that sex, when done right, can unlock the creative genius in a woman. It's worth a try, isn't it? Next time you're feeling stuck on a project and perhaps frustrated and at your wit's end, schedule a sex date with your husband to help relax your body, unclog your mind and get your creative juices flowing again.

PHYSICAL BONDING AND SPIRITUAL AWAKENING

This one may come as a surprise but be rest assured that the more you have sex with your spouse, the closer you are bound to be. Knowing this; approach sex with a lot more excitement and perhaps a glow in your eyes. Your husband will love it for sure, and it'll make for an even more exciting experience for you. Oxytocin is a hormone released during orgasm and can be responsible for the feelings of closeness and bonding after sex. In fact, studies show that a woman's brain continues to release oxytocin even after sex, longer than men, which may explain why we just love to continue cuddling even after the sex is over.

In some cases, one may feel generally lighter and better able to connect during praise and worship after sex. There is a reason some women scream, Praise God and other funny things during an orgasm, and it is nothing to be embarrassed about. We are experiencing something beautiful with someone we love and it is okay to bring gratitude to God, the creator of all beautiful experiences. This may sound corny but it really isn't. If you like, you can feel free to even burst into a song or a prayer session right after a memorable love-making session. It may be funny at first, but when sex is done between two adults in a marriage, it makes it easier to be vulnerable with each other and embark on a spiritual journey together. There should be no judgment or shame in our matrimonial bed, so let us blush less and learn to be free with the husband of our youth.

PROCREATION

This is perhaps the most popular purpose for marriage. Having sex for procreation is an instinctual practice. Research suggests that if we make sex a boring and strict routine only to be had when we ovulate simply because we are trying to conceive, the anxiety presented may actually be counterproductive and make it harder to get pregnant. So while it is important to know our cycle and anticipate our ovulation, we can try to also have sex at other times so we do not become overwhelmed with anxiety. It may help to distract ourselves a little by focusing on the different other purposes of sex even when we are trying to conceive. When we finally get pregnant, I hear that it is okay to continue to enjoy sex, as pregnancy should not be a barrier to sex, unless our doctor advises otherwise for health reasons. You may sign up for ante-natal as soon as you can, so that you and your baby receive the best possible medical care and attention.

There are several books on how a woman can maintain peace in her home, so feel free to consult these resources or speak to trusted and qualified individuals if you have any concerns about your relationship with your spouse. Although marriage exists between two people from different backgrounds, with different personalities and love languages, I believe marriage can, and should be enjoyed.

There are beautiful marriages and even if we do not hear about them every day, we will find some beautiful couples around us if we pay close attention. I am hopeful that your marriage will be everything you dreamed possible and more. And yes, it is okay to dream about marriage and look forward to a happy-ever-after. You deserve this.

7.4 WORKPLACE RELATIONSHIPS

If you are concerned about maintaining a good relationship with your colleagues at work, whether they are your bosses or subordinates, here are a few tips to help you maintain professionalism while pursuing a satisfactory career progression.

1. Build ethics appropriate for your type and place of work. Workplace ethics can be pretty great at helping you keep a level head in your relationships at work. So find out what the ethics of your work include and work hard to uphold those ethics. Some workplaces extol honesty, integrity, transparency, timeliness etc. What matters to a hospital may not be what matters to a hospitality business like a hotel. It is our duty to know what our office is about.

2. Use work appropriate language. When relating with clients and colleagues, use the acceptable language of communication. Some workplaces allow only a certain type of language, English for instance while some other offices do not mind a mix of the official language with other non-formal varieties. Again, be advised of the office preferred language and communicate accordingly. Do not use profane or vulgar languages, especially at work and of course do your best to be civil in your communication and conduct.

3. Observe personal hygiene. If you prioritize your personal grooming, chances are that you will be easier to relate with and people are more likely to be excited at the prospect of having you as part of their team for a group project. Nobody wants to sit next to the colleague who always has bad breath and smells badly all the time. This may seem like a no-brainer but you would be shocked how much some people ignore their personal hygiene and just show up to work looking and smelling anyhow. No matter where you work, make it a practice to always show up looking clean and tidy. If you suspect you may have stale breath, suck on a breath mint or use a portable mouth wash before talking to a colleague or client. These things happen so there's no need to be embarrassed even when someone else points it out, simply do the needful. Use a decent-smelling soap and take time to have a thorough bath as often as you need to. Invest in deodorants and perfumes, being careful to avoid obnoxious fragrances and wear the mildest perfumes, when necessary.

4. Dress the way you want to be addressed. Workplace fashion is so essential to workplace relationships. Every employer wants to hire someone that looks decent. At least, that is one thing I always consider when I'm part of a recruitment team. You do not have to wear the most expensive outfits to dress smart. Simply iron your clothes and pay attention to how you match colors, fabrics and patterns. And pick out work clothes that compliment your body type and agree with your place of work. Even if you are unsure what is best, it is okay to ask someone for tips or even ask one of your girlfriends to go shopping with you next time. If there is a dress code, follow it. I have been able to access some of the most elite conferences and corporate events as well as social events, partly because I try my best to pay attention to my wardrobe and have worked with different stylists over the years in my work as an event host. Even at my Hosting Academy, one of the courses is on style because fashion speaks volume in our work as women. I have also collaborated with fashion creators to create incredible work outfits at my fashion brand, Raylivia, to make workplace fashion a much easier thing to navigate for the modern woman. Do not be in the habit of wearing tight fitting and short dresses if your office requires coveralls and do not wear coveralls when you are expected to dress smart. Grab a jacket if you know you work in a cold environment instead of shivering and rubbing your shoulder all day or borrowing your colleagues' jackets always. There will always be time for casual dresses so dress appropriately to work. A banker and a mixologist have different expectations of dressing both by their office and the clients they serve. Respect the dress code.

5. Be firm but polite. You do not want to come off as difficult to work with but at the same time you do not want to become a doormat at work. Practice saying no in front of the mirror if you need to, because there are some people who you need to say no to from time to time in your workplace. If you are not firm, chances are, people may take advantage of you. But even in being firm, also realize that part of being a team player is being nice and polite, so know when to strategically offer a yes to the right persons for the greater good of the team. We discussed being a team player and navigating office politics in chapter 4 of this book and I believe that captures the essence of workplace relationships. You are better served if your bosses and colleagues like working with you, so do your best to be nice at work, within reason. Sometimes, the most efficient workers are passed over during promotions and rewards and the most sociable take their place. This won't be you if you master the art of balancing efficiency and sociability. Sharpen your social networking skills and do your best to be the one the team can't let go of if there's ever a downsizing. Smile and be friendly, but do not be anybody's doormat.

6. Respect boundaries. Last but certainly not least, you must create boundaries for yourself that dictate what you allow and enforce same. If you know that you do not entertain workplace romance, then create and enforce some clear rules that depict that. As a matter of professionalism, some work places do not even entertain workplace romance, so be discreet if you even begin any such relationships for whatever reason. If you meet someone you like at work, and you are convinced that you will be great together forever, then keep it private and away from work until you are both ready to make your wedding announcements. In most offices, one person may be asked to resign and you can carry on with your marriage. Trust me, even if your office has no clearly stated rules against workplace dating, you are better served to create personal boundaries that protect you so that if the relationship doesn't work out, you can nurse your heartbreak in peace, without suffering the extra humiliation of your colleagues teasing you or speculating. There is no point in jeopardizing your work relationship for a romantic relationship that may not work out, so keep it private.

If you want to advance a work place relationship to a platonic friendship, and you think that one of your colleagues or clients will make a good friend, then first ensure that you are not breaking any company policies in so doing. Once this is ascertained, make your request known to the person using the pattern we discussed earlier in this chapter on how to make friends.

7.5 SPIRITUALITY

And now these three remain: faith, hope and love. But the greatest of these is love. **- I Corinthians 13:13 (NIV).** This quote from a letter that the Apostle Paul wrote to Christians in Corinth is such a powerful reminder of the ultimate nature of Love. In my years on earth, I have found a love so strong and so compelling, that it keeps me going even on my weakest days. It is most commonly referred to as Agape Love, the purest form of unconditional love. As we discuss the matter of relationships, let us look at a personal relationship with our creator.

Building Intimacy with God

I grew up in a Christian home and so I assumed that automatically meant that I knew God and had a relationship with him. But at some point in my life, living life based on what my Church leaders and parents told me about God wasn't just enough anymore. I wanted to experience him for myself and I couldn't quite understand how I could make sense of a God who I couldn't see or talk to but somehow I was hopeful that the stories I heard from people who claimed to have a relationship with God would come to be in my life, because some things in life just didn't make sense to my young mind and I wanted clarity.

One day, a little while after I had given my life to Christ, at the brink of a most hurtful breakup, one of my friends jokingly suggested that I ask God to come and be my friend and fill the big space and emptiness I felt in my heart and perhaps I would find the fulfillment I had been searching for in a man. It had come off as a joke but I was desperate to experience a genuine relationship with a loving God, if he existed. And so I asked God to please be my friend and I can't fully explain how that simple heart cry has been heard and answered over and over again. And so the journey to building an intimate relationship with God began for me. Over the years, I have grown from experiencing a relationship with God as my friend to even embracing him as my father, healer, protector and ultimate provider.

Personally, it hasn't been the easiest journey for me, getting over the human disappointments, work stress, relationship palaver and all the other cares of life, and truly embracing the possibility of a loving God who found me worthy to die for. Sometimes I allow my perception of humans and past experiences to create doubt in my heart but somehow the love of God reaches out into the depth of my doubts and troubles and pulls me up to a place of restoration and healing.

The most important relationship I have discovered is a personal relationship with God, who knows the good, the bad and the ugly about me, but loves me regardless. In the midst of every self-doubt, or fear or trial or disappointment, I just hear him say everything will be fine and it keeps me going.

Some of the most important life decisions for me concerning my career, choice of a spouse, and everyday human relationships have been made clearer and much easier to navigate through the loving guidance of the Holy Spirit. And I have risen from some of my biggest failures and disappointment simply because God's love held me. There are some times we get to a crossroad and we don't even know the next path to take, but there's that still small voice inside pointing us in the right direction. I'll share one such experience in raising my daughter. At some point, I realized she was a bit more restless and would often interrupt my conversations with my husband, her grandma, and others more than she used to do. It bothered me so much. One day I decided to simply ask God for a way out. My prayer was more like a conversation as I asked God what I may have been doing wrong and if there was something I could do to help my daughter be more understanding of the need for privacy and boundaries in certain adult interactions. I did not bother to ask God why my child was acting in that way because I had learned that most times, when I go to God pushing all the blame to the other party, I don't often get a response until I am willing to take personal responsibility in the solution I seek. So I asked God if there was something I was doing or wasn't doing that may have produced such behavior. The answer I got in prayer was simple yet practical. I realized I wasn't giving her enough personal time like I used to and so she was simply acting out because of the lack of attention. It was nothing too deep, but yet it was very important for me because I really didn't know what else I would have done to turn things around.

As simple as fun baths, dancing time, exercise time, baking time and cycling time etc, I try to be deliberate about creating precious moments with her, even doing mundane activities, that we both will cherish forever. The result is a daughter who allows me my own time with others knowing that she and I share our own uninterrupted special moments. As I enjoyed the success of this simple shift in our relationship, I started to extend this same principle to my other relationships, including my relationship with my husband. This simple strategy that I got from a prayer made in all honesty to a loving father has saved me a lot of headache in my home. In the same way, there are so many other instances were a simple prayer or seeking God's opinion on a matter no matter how frivolous has given me wonderful results and strategies for my business and personal life.

And while many people argue the existence of an all knowing, all loving God, I simply wonder what my life would have been without my hope and faith. We mustn't allow anybody mock us for our belief in God, because somewhere deep within every one of us, there is this desire for a deep connection, and hope, faith and love are all we have on some days to really keep us going.

> **For a truly holistic living experience for a woman, I strongly recommend a relationship with God, the one who has been from the very beginning.**

Have you ever wondered why irrespective of everything you have been through in life, you are still alive? Whether you're happy or sad, rich or poor, anxious or excited, single or married, you are still alive here on earth. Well, I wonder it too. I have survived an abduction and robbery that nearly made me an anxious mess, and painful miscarriages, with so many other curve balls life keep throwing my way but somehow, I am still alive and hopeful for one more day. Every day that I wake up is a gift and I choose to look at it that way, because somehow someway, I am convinced that my life is not an accident and I am here on earth by a deliberate design of a loving creator.

I have summarized some of these things that are helping me build an intimate relationship with God. I sincerely hope that they can help you too.

1. Have a little faith: To even begin a relationship with God, just like with humans, we do have to desire the relationship and have some faith that He exists. *'And without faith it is impossible to please God, because anyone who comes to him must believe that he exists and that he rewards those who earnestly seek him.'* - Hebrews 11:6 (NIV)

We can say a simple prayer and invite God into our life to begin an intimate relationship with him. Then trust him enough to talk with him through prayer and to seek to know him through study of his word. I won't even pretend like it is a straightforward journey but I think what helps is knowing that it is okay to fall and rise again. Perhaps the verse that can give us confidence that God reciprocates when we reach out to him for a relationship would be where James says to, ***draw near to God and he will draw near to us***.

2. Keep hope alive: Relationships can be a bit sensitive whether with humans and with God so perhaps we can keep an open mind and stay hopeful in our relationship with God. Just like when we desire a relationship with someone and we don't allow any false things we've heard about them discourage us from seeing for ourselves, especially if it's someone we have a crush on. Sometimes we find out they're actually the real deal and other times we find out they're not There are times when absolutely nothing makes sense but somehow hope in our heart will keep us going each new day. I found this scripture on hope at one of the lowest points in my life and it really encouraged me.

"At least there is hope for a tree: If it is cut down, it will sprout again, and its new shoots will not fail. Its roots may grow old in the ground and its stump die in the soil, yet at the scent of water it will bud and put forth shoots like a plant." **- (Job 14:7-9).**

3. Walk in love: Sometimes the greatest hindrance to a beautiful relationship with God can be the limitations of our own relationship with others. Because God is love, I suppose he finds it very attractive when we also walk in Love. I like to imagine that love takes us from zero to hundred real quick in our relationship with God. And what is Love? *Love is patient, love is kind. It does not envy, it does not boast, it is not proud. It does not dishonour others, it is not self-seeking, it is not easily angered, and it keeps no record of wrongs.* **(1 Corinthians 13:4-8)**

Initially I had thought the Holy Spirit was reserved for a few special believers but over the years, I have learned to simply believe God's word when He says the Holy Spirit is a free gift given to every believer. It has to be, otherwise how would we even begin to practice love for all. Love can sound so cool until we are asked to show that love to a hater. Living a Christian life is a sure struggle without the Holy Spirit.

'And hope does not put us to shame, because God's love has been poured out into our hearts through the Holy Spirit, who has been given to us.' **- Romans 5:5 (NIV).**

So my hope is that God will give us the grace to live a life of love in our relationship with our own selves and with others, on the good days and on the bad days.

On our journey to holistic living, we need these relationships to enjoy a balance in our personal, work and social life. So here's to a fun filled life, sprinkled with the most beautiful relationships and most fruitful networks possible.

Love heals the chancre of long rejection.
It is with a kiss or a long warm hug.
Ears wide open, and hearts of affection.
Filling all emptiness rejection dug.

Love kills, yet it be not one of its flaws.
Here, it punctuates a sad maiden's dialect.
It's the death in a mother lion's steel claws.
Her wet cubs against foe beasts to protect.

Love steals, away, strength to do as you please.
Fills up the graveyard of old days' romance.
The umbilical cord of tomorrow's bliss.
If you find her easy, it's in a trance.

The frail miss hurts the hunk with this old tool.
Love is sweetest when you're loved by a fool.
Love Heals – **Ray Anyasi**

CHAPTER 8
PERSONAL ECONOMICS

Chrissy was the official hype woman of the group and even as the ladies crossed the Kakum Canopy Walk. She was still chirping away happily hyping each lady and filming the entire experience on her camcorder. Halfway across the canopy, everyone had gone quiet, they were now in the thick of the forest and any wrong footing could result in broken limbs and shattered hopes. Lara had vehemently refused to get on the canopy walk. Her fear of heights had come as a big surprise to every one of the ladies who had come to know her as fearless in all things.

Lara the Great was scared of heights and commitments. She had called off her engagement two months to the wedding and seemed even happier to be single again. As usual, she was not going to tell anyone what made her change her mind and was just happy that Jide let her keep her engagement ring. She had tried to sell it off on Ebay, but after she learnt it was not worth as much as she was led to believe, she decided to keep the ring as a memorabilia, which made her breakup even the more ominous.

Did she really call it off or was that just her cover-up story to mask her pain?

The ladies couldn't tell for sure and nobody wanted to confront Lara the Great. Nobody could even dare, except of, course Adjoa, whose lavish home the five ladies had now made their home for the past few days on their exciting vacation. She was truly wealthier than they had projected, perhaps even more than all four of them combined.

Adjoa caught her breath sharply and made to catch the falling camcorder as Chrissy waved her hands in the air excitedly as she stepped on to the other end of the canopy walk. Too late, the camcorder hit a rock as it slid down all the way to the bottom.

In the most surprising manner, Chrissy turned to the bridge and bade a hesitant farewell to the camcorder as she burst into delirious laughter. Adjoa had never met such a free spirited woman before. Nothing seemed to move Chrissy, this 28 year old mother who she was most drawn to on this trip. This reaction particularly touched her, especially after the heartwarming story Chrissy had told on their ride that morning about the camcorder being a graduation gift from her dad. It held so many beautiful memories of her closely knit family and her son's first three years. But she was sure there was a backup somewhere. That could only explain the carefree way Chrissy continued to attack her gum and blow big bubbles in the air.

Back home at the Nana Mansion, dinner was set waiting for the ladies to return. They saw a side of Adjoa that screamed royalty and class. She seemed too young for the height of the 3 children who filed out to greet her, welcome mother. Her first son was 16 while the girls were 12 and 10 respectively. And they looked so alike it was as though they were *déjàvu* copies of one another. Adjoa sat at the head of the table and the children all found joy taking off her shoes and jewelry. She signaled for one of the maids who brought hot towels for each of the ladies to wipe their hands after washing. Dinner was a simple buffet of different varieties. There was banku and banga with tilapia fish, as well as shitor sauce to go along. In honor of her Nigerian guests she had asked the chef to surprise them with something spectacular. Buogo was the first to yell, Isiewu, excitedly when she got to the table, and then Chrissy made everybody wait until she took photos of every deliciousness on the table before they sat to eat. She was a Youtuber on the side, any and everything was great content that she made money from.

Later that evening, they all sat around to listen to cool music from a saxophonist at the terrace after a soulful massage session. Everything was going rather well on this vacation, Adjoa thought. When she moved to Nigeria a year ago to find herself, she had not imagined that she would return home with four of the most dynamic young ladies she had ever met. Every one of them had a story but somehow they seemed to have found a way to live in the present and let go of the past. She found it utterly refreshing and their lives had inspired her to give her marriage another chance. Her husband was worth it, after pulling the stunt he did when he came to find her in Nigeria unannounced, she was finally ready to stop running and come back to fight for everything she ever worked for and all she ever wanted; her children, her marriage, and her pageantry training school for young girls.

The ladies all looked at Adjoa from time to time as she pulled mindlessly on her knotless braids. Everybody was waiting for her big revelation. They had each agreed to share the story of their happiest and saddest days ever and how it has made them the women they are. They had chosen the canopy walk as a symbolic exercise to confront their inner fears. Suddenly the saxophonist stopped playing and the ladies gave her the widest smiles in affirmation. Chrissy went all in, screaming her own affirmation and throwing kisses in the air. When the giggles and applause simmered off, all eyes turned to Adjoa. There was nowhere to run in that moment, it was her turn to share as the host and the initiator of the sharing circle. She opened her mouth to start and instead of the expected, she blurted out the one thing that had been on her mind all day.

"Ladies, I think I'm pregnant!"

To be continued.

THE MAKING OF THE HOLISTIC WOMAN

****

Economics is a science that studies human behaviour as a relationship between ends and scarce means which have alternative uses. Of all definitions of economics by different philosophers and social scientists in history, this definition by Lionel Robbins is the one that comes readily to my mind as I navigate this *baby-girl* lifestyle that I have committed to living. I am always grateful to my parents as well as my lecturers and classmates for the chance to study Economics at the University of Nigeria, because in many ways this social science has given me a deeper appreciation for life.

What do I wear today? How much should I spend on my new hair and bag? Should I hang-out with my sister or spend the day catching up on extra work for that bonus check? Should I let my children play outside with the neighbours or give them an iPad to play indoors? Can I afford a vacation this year or should I buy land instead? Should I call my new flame or just pay him a surprise visit? Do I have enough time to make a proper meal or should I just microwave the pizza from last night? Karaoke with the ladies or stay home and do laundry? How do I lose weight and still remain a certified foodie? Should I spend time in thanksgiving to God or rush out for evangelism? Can I afford to have a baby now or wait till after my Master's program? Should I book a couple's massage for our wedding anniversary or splurge on the latest Victoria's Secret lingerie and give hubby a lap-dance instead? Should I sleep now or catch one more episode of Numbers. The list is endless. So many beautiful options and things to consider.

What's a girl to do? The truth remains that as women, we are always faced with choices and we're always making decisions based on our sentiments and judgment however emotional or logical they may be. So it is safe to say that we are already practicing Economics even if we do not know it. Wants, needs, scale of preference, opportunity cost, and choices are some economic principles that are part of our everyday lives. We have unlimited wants and needs but limited time, and resources to satisfy them all at the same time. So in order to enjoy a flawlessly pampered lifestyle, we must seek to understand what matters most to us per time and focus on those things, while doing our best to ensure that we have the resources to satisfy these wants and needs. We have looked at different liberating concepts in this book so far but yet we know that for us as women to enjoy an integrated lifestyle where we eat what is best for us, exercise our body and mind, enjoy a satisfactory work, have some good fun, as well as connect with our loved ones, we must have the means available to us. So in this chapter, let us take a bold and daring dive as we explore how the modern woman can create a vision for her life, as well as ways to ultimately achieve financial independence while being content at whatever level she finds herself in her life's journey. Let's discuss the Personal Economics of a modern woman.

8.1 ON PURPOSE, VISION AND FINDING FULFILLMENT

We discussed work in Chapter 4 of this book, and while I know that work can give a woman a sense of relevance, I also understand that not every woman finds satisfaction in her chosen work. And this is why many of us struggle even in a job that is financially rewarding, but unfulfilling.

More often than not, the reason is simply because we may have chosen a job based on the wrong reasons and with no clear purpose and vision in mind. And when the purpose of a thing is not clearly defined, abuse is inevitable. Why do we do what we do?

A few years ago, I met a missionary, during one of my outreaches and capacity building initiatives, Everybody Deserves a Merry Christmas. Pastor Walt Troupe lived with his wife and his teenage daughter in a Village in Opi, Nsukka, in West Africa. He was father to 73 children who had come to the Place of Hope Orphanage for refuge. These were young children and teenagers who had run to the orphanage for shelter because they were displaced during war or other crisis in their own countries and regions. Some of the children were simply abandoned by their parents close to the orphanage while some were orphans who had lost their parents in accidents and sickness and had resorted to begging on the streets and petty theft. Pastor Walt and his family had left their family and friends and all the comfort of their native country and moved to Africa to be a family to these vulnerable children. They ate together, prayed together and were one big happy family. It amazed me so greatly the way that the children all called him daddy. They looked at peace in the new life they had chosen, and even though they did not have everything, they shared the little they had and seemed content. Most of the children went to school in the village and were taken care of by this family, the few staff they had and the older children in the orphanage. In the years that I interacted with them, I could always sense a profound joy and peace that seemed to radiate all around the orphanage home. As we do for orphanages in our program, we provided medical care, as well as educational tools, food and clothing to these young ones. However, it is the physical time my friends and I spent driving all the way from the city to their orphanage home to play football, enjoy their cultural dance, engage in all sorts of singing competition and all other sorts of fun that forms some of the most beautiful memories in my mind and in the mind of my friends. Beyond giving them material resources, we shared our time with the children and I suppose this helped them feel more like a relevant part of society.

The purpose of a thing is the reason why it is created. This simple definition points to the fact that an understanding of our purpose as women will help us pursue a meaningful life that we will find enjoyable and fulfilling. So when I wonder why Pastor Troupe and his wife would leave the comfort of their country and live in a foreign land just to be a family to those who do not have one, I figure it is the same reason that would make my friends and I travel a long way and put funds together to bring Everybody Deserves a Merry Christmas to these children. We seem to find a sense of fulfillment in sharing our life and gifts with others.

Over the years I have facilitated at several teen and youth camps as well as women conventions where everyone seems interested and eager to find an answer to the ultimate question, *what is my purpose?*

I often refer to finding our SHAPE to try to answer the question of purpose for myself and others because just as our shapes are different, so are our individual purposes. The SHAPE concept was developed by Rick Warren, in his bestselling book, Purpose Driven Life, and is an acronym for SPIRITUAL GIFTS, HEART, ABILITY, PERSONALITY AND EXPERIENCES. An understanding of our SHAPE will point us in the right direction and help us make the decisions that will matter most in the short term and long run. No matter our age in life, it is never too late to find and walk in our purpose. This is how I recommend we find our SHAPE.

1. SPIRITUAL GIFTS: Some people have the gift of faith, believing everything is possible. Compassion, wisdom and knowledge etc are all spiritual gifts that we possess in

different measures so take note of yours. One does not struggle in her spiritual gifts.

2. HEART: what moves our heart, what does our heart beat for, what makes us very angry? what makes us cry? Injustice? Poverty? Child abuse? Quality service? Excellence? Governance? Technological innovation? whatever moves our heart is most likely something we have the natural inclination to address.

3. ABILITY: what are we naturally good at? Can we effortlessly make people laugh? Do we understand patterns and colors? Do numbers excite us? And do we climb heights that others fear? The answers will point to our natural abilities.

4. PERSONALITY: what is our natural disposition? Are we shy, bold, easily angry, good with people, talkative, very articulate, internally motivated, analytical, etc. Our personality often points to our purpose. This is not to excuse bad behaviour and bask in our weaknesses. If we Identify our natural strengths and weaknesses, we can improve on them. If we expect that others will accommodate our weaknesses, just remember that the law will not excuse hitting a colleague as mere hot-temper, but will prosecute. So we have to work on our weaknesses, and do what we can to improve. If we gravitate towards the things that our personality makes us a good fit for, we will most likely be happy in it.

5. EXPERIENCE: whatever we've been through and truly overcome is what we've become empowered to influence. Whether our experiences involve negative or positive occurrences like rape, financial independence, childhood trauma, discrimination, self confidence, smooth pregnancy, successful career, etc., we are most likely better equipped

and positioned to handle issues that we have been through and overcome. Some experiences can be rather hurtful and painful when we go through them as women but somehow, if we persist and find healing, then we become great at helping others win in that area. If we have overcome a negative experience, it may be easier for us to help prevent others from going through that ugly incidence or help protect others in vulnerable positions, as well as help those who have gone through such an experience find healing in the ways that we did. Again, our positive experiences are a refreshing force for good. If we have tried and proven successful in an area of our life, we stand a great chance of being able to guide others through that path. Experiences can also be drawn from our past academic and educational qualifications as well as all work experiences.

> **We are more likely to find our work satisfactory and enjoyable, irrespective of the dynamics at play and the remuneration if we pursue a work in line with our purpose.**

Do not go on a wild goose chase in the name of trying to find purpose in life. If this SHAPE course leaves more questions in your heart than answers, then simply be content with living your life each day, showing love to the people around you and taking care of yourself as much as possible while doing the work you find. In due time, your purpose and vision will be clear to you if you get up every day and keep going.

Never lose hope or think it is all over because you feel like your life lacks direction and meaning. As long as we're alive, we matter and we're relevant. Perhaps we should turn to God in our moment of confusion since the purpose of anything is best defined by its creator. The fact that a child uses a TV remote as a drumstick doesn't change the purpose of that TV remote from being a device for navigating content on TV screen to a sound instrument. And the fact that we only use our phone to make and receive calls does not stop it from being a device worthy of much more functions. If we read the manual of every product, we will find the original purpose the creator intended for that product. So, to find our own purpose, we can look to our creator and harness our SHAPE. Refer to Chapter 7 of this book where we discussed how to build a relationship with God, as a map to connect to our creator for clarity on our purpose. Even if we have been abused in different ways in the past, our value and worth is preserved deep within us. And even in instances where we may have been the one that subjected our own lives to unimaginable things, we are still worthy of love and there is value inside us. Any day we wake up and decide that we have had enough, and take back charge of our life and future, we may be surprised to find what power is within us and the great heights we can reach.

Having a Vision is simply the ability to think about or plan our future in line with the purpose we have identified for our lives. Having a vision is an indication that we have a clear sense of purpose. And so our purpose will drive us to write out a vision for our life and to break down that vision into achievable goals. We may desire to be the best mother possible, an astrophysicist, a great chef, a caring nurse, a philanthropist, a disruptor, the kindest wife, the most helpful neighbor, a writer, a pilot, a physician, an innovative farmer or simply a happy person. A vision does not have to be complicated or overly ambitious to matter. It is okay to be unique and simple in our vision. Whoever we choose to be and whatever we choose to do, the choice is ours.

One effective way that we can articulate our vision, goals and dreams is to keep a vision board.

A vision board is can help us focus on our goals in the long and short term. We can write on our vision board or clip items on it that remind us what really matters to us to keep us inspired so that we don't lose our faith or focus.

Here are a few tips for a vision board.

1. Make goals clear and smart by writing it down on the vision board. A goal is considered SMART when it is Specific, Measurable, Achievable, Realistic and with a Time Frame.

2. Prioritize goals to help delegate time and resources properly. We can have money goals, friendship goals, exercise goals, weight goals, spiritual goals, academic goals, character goals, vacation goals, nutrition goals, sleep goals etc. Some things matter more than others in the short run while some matter more in the long run, so we may reflect the order of priority on our vision board. For instance, a new mum may want to prioritize rest and relaxation over work while a grad student may want to prioritize study time. The priority of one woman is to be a good mother by investing in her self-care while the priority of the other woman is to make good grades by investing in her self-development. At any point in time, our priorities can change in response to our situations and should therefore be reflected in our vision board as they do.

3. Find images and words that resonate with our vision and clip it on the vision board. We can even make sketches or doodles as we like. Our vision board is private and personal, so, we can feel free to include the things that make us happy. A newspaper clipping of the countries we want to travel to, a picture of our father to remind us where we're from, or even a cutout from a magazine that features our favorite food to help us eat well every day. I am still trying to figure out the best way to include water on my vision

board to make me drink more water every day. However silly or intense an item is, as long as they are relevant to our journey, they belong on our vision board.

4. Keep the vision board within sight. We want it to be somewhere we can always see it. Some good suggestions are by the bedside so we can see it when we get up in the morning, on the bathroom wall, on the fridge door or even at the office. Some people put theirs on the phone and just have a digital vision board.

5. Always feel free to arrange and rearrange the vision board to reflect any changes in plans. We can even put positive affirmations on our vision board as well as records of our little wins and successes to motivate ourselves on our life journey.

Would you be creating a vision board? I sure hope so.

8.2 FINANCIAL INDEPENDENCE - HOW TO FUND AND MAINTAIN THE LIFESTYLE YOU DESIRE

Now that we have decided how to set our vision and goals for life, there are some systems and structures we can put in place to ensure we meet these visions and goals even as we maximize our present resources. It is important that we continue to prioritize our own physical, emotional and mental health as we strive to fulfill our dreams. To get to a place of true financial independence, a woman would need to have enough resources to live the life she desires today and tomorrow. For the longest time this particular topic has been on my mind, first for myself and then for others. How can a woman truly ever be financially independent, especially when she is still expected to be a wife, friend, daughter, sister, mother and still take care of her own self? Let us consider some ways to ensure this financial independence becomes more attainable for us as women.

Budget

It may seem odd to learn about how we can properly budget the money we make even when we may not even have any money to budget yet. I have deliberately put this particular horse right in front of the proverbial cart where it belongs because I believe that the reason we don't have enough money to do the things that really matter to us as women when the need arises is because sometimes we do not decide what we need the money for before we even get it. So once we get money, we just rush and do the first things that come to our mind without even thinking about it logically. So, let's say we get a bonus 100 dollars now, what is the first thing we would do with it? We may simply buy the first thing that catches our attention on our way back from the bank or give the money to the first person that comes to tell us a sad story of their predicament if we don't have any plans for our income, and in so doing, we remain at one particular level such that when it is time to give ourselves a treat, take care of a medical emergency, further our education, pamper a loved one, or expand our business, we find that we may begin to struggle. It is safe to say that sometimes we fail to succeed in our quest for financial independence because we do not have any plan of how to spend the money that we make or that we receive as gifts. Not anymore.

I struggled in my personal finances for a long time because of this very thing and sometimes when I save enough to put towards a car or invest, I would simply use the personal funds to help those less privileged through my McOlivia Foundation. And I know that I am not alone because I have heard so many stories from other women who find it hard to resist the urge to do good for others at their own expense. Charity is good but should begin with us doing some charity for our own selves, so that we would be well enough to do for others. After a few years doing this haphazard emotional charity that left me with very little funds to build my life in a way I could make bigger impact, I decided to change strategy and look ahead. One year I saved up some good money and decided to register my NGO instead, a process that took a period of 4 long years but eventually worked. Becoming a registered entity helped me put structure in place in a way that I could access better help for the indigent, the underprivileged and the vulnerable in society for whom I have great passion, so my desire to help is satisfied when I see others truly taken care of through my foundation. This way, I am learning to be a bit more disciplined in my personal finances by creating systems and structures that guide me so that I can administer my income judiciously. In the end, everybody wins; both those I am trying to help and myself.

My sister-in-law, Ojiugo, always reminds me of a saying that I love, which is that one cannot pour from an empty cup. So when we prioritize Self-care, we are better able to take care of others around us. That way, we are fine and our loved ones are fine too. Most of us grew up watching our parents sacrifice so much for others that we have adopted it even in greater measure. But we must not continue to self-sabotage because we refuse to plan. Instead of always sacrificing our own growth and happiness for everyone else to be happy while we stay miserable, we can create a budget.

Creating a budget, can help us plan how we will spend our money even before we get it so that once we get that bank alert, we already know what we will use the money for, and which part will go towards savings, helping others, i.e, charity, investments, our education, our own enjoyment, pampering our loved ones and so forth. It is easier to plan for our income before we receive it than after we have received it. Since we have decided the things that matter to us in the long run, we can consciously start saving and investing towards them, and the things that matter most to us in the short run, we can spend on now.

Here are some basic components that can make up a budget for the modern woman.

1. SAVINGS: If we would have enough savings for the rainy day, we need to apply discipline to remove our savings to avoid being overwhelmed by so many expenses once we start spending that we forget to save. The money we save can go towards funding our dream of owning a home someday or our rent at the end of the year, buying a car or any such needs.

2. INVESTMENTS: To invest is to set aside some funds for the purchase of an asset or process with the hope that it will generate further income or appreciate in value at some point in the future. So we can set aside parts of our income to invest in the expansion of an already existing business or invest in real-estate, stock market, bonds, mutual funds, etc. Buying a car is considered an asset but it is not an investment because its value depreciates over time while an investment has to be something that appreciates in value, except in rare cases where the car is a vintage and actually appreciates in value, but that's an exception, not the rule. Money we invest now can go towards our retirement funds or an education fund for us or our loved ones or affording luxuries like a yacht or travelling the world or setting up a facility for cancer-care, etc., any time in our future as we see fit. We can fund our dreams, both big and small with a good investment, as long as we give it time. Every woman can invest towards a better future and Robert Kiyosaki argues in his book, Cashflow Quadrant, that becoming an investor is an awesome way to attain

financial freedom, where we can continue to enjoy the lifestyle we desire without depending on a monthly paycheck. We may get some expert advice as there are different types of investments for everyone and some are relatively safer than others while some offer more returns than others. We can learn quite a lot about investments on the Internet and in books if we cannot afford the services of a financial adviser/advisor. The choice of when, how, and what to invest on is ultimately ours.

3. RECURRING EXPENSES: Recurring expenses include some of our needs that must be met on a regular basis. Things like utility bills, grocery shopping and the money that goes into our day-to-day essentials like food, clothing, hygiene products, basic medical supplies, transportation, electricity and water bills, etc. This will probably be the biggest expenses we make on a monthly basis but once we find that we are spending more money on certain things than our income can cover, then we may consider cutting down on those things to avoid going completely broke. Like they say, we would need to cut our coat according to our cloth. If we find out that the body spray we use keeps getting more expensive every day, then we may look for a more affordable brand to patronize if our income is not also growing in that period. Sometimes certain products are more expensive, not because they are necessarily better in quality but simply because of the color of the packaging and other mundane factors. Hygiene products in pink packages generally cost more than the ones in blue packages. So a pack of shaving stick that is blue in colour may be sold for 1 dollar while a pack of shaving stick that is pink in color may be sold for 3 dollars. Logic would dictate that we choose the more affordable product since they do the same work and offer the same result and are made by the same manufacturer sometimes.

There is something called Pink Tax where women products are priced higher than men products just because brands and government understand our sentimental attachment to certain shapes and colors. If one can afford it, then sure, she may use products that have pink colors and are targeted at women, but if she cannot honestly afford them, she may simply buy the more affordable options as long as the content is the same anyway. Let's stay woke ladies. Lawmakers in several states in the United States have successfully advocated for the elimination of the Tampon Tax, another price discrimination that makes menstrual products more expensive than other products in their category. So, as modern women in these days and times, we may be better served to change to a more affordable hygiene product than to continue increasing the cost of purchasing a particular brand thereby reducing the money we have available for other expenses or even overworking ourselves chasing these shadows.

4. PERSONAL DEVELOPMENT: This is the money we set aside for developing ourselves in any area of our life we want to improve and learn. Improving oneself can help to directly increase one's earning potential. It is important to deliberately set aside funds for our personal development. We set money aside so that as the need arises, we are able to afford Books, attend relevant trainings and certifications, get a Master's degree, or PhD or for the education of our wards. This is essential for career advancement, emotional as well as spiritual growth and shows that we value ourselves enough to keep manifesting new and improved versions of ourselves. It's okay if we are new at a job, or we're a new mum, or new wife or new car owner or new volleyball player, but a little investment in our personal development will improve our capacity. Sometimes all we may need is a good book on the subject matter to provide us the basic knowledge we need to apply to be better and earn better. Depending on our goals and income, we can choose the best options for personal development at

every point in time. For instance, you can find a lot of free courses on Coursera and other online platforms and even YouTube can teach you some basic and advanced things ranging from how to style your daughter's hair for a birthday party to how to build an investment portfolio or how to design a website or how to cook Nigerian Jollof rice. The Internet has made learning more affordable these days, so if you want to learn data science, you may subscribe to a course on Udemy or apply for a degree program in a university. You will get the same knowledge at different prices and with different certifications. So depending on your education goal and funds available, you will be able to choose wisely. At any level of financial earning, we should be deliberate about investing in our personal development because it will make a difference in our quality of life in the long run. Additionally, you can invest a little extra time to find scholarships available for your personal development. As an Economist, I have always been passionate about Human Capital Development as a key to a better society and this led me to do my degree project on the topic of Human Capital Development and its impact on Economic Growth, using the Health and Education indices for measuring Human Capital Development. My research indicates that when we commit to a good overall health and education, we raise our general quality of life and ability to create wealth which in turn impacts positively on society. So as we keep taking the responsibility for developing ourselves, the possibilities for holistic living are limitless.

5. SELF-CARE: This is basically an aspect of our income that we set aside to ensure that we continue to take care of ourselves and enjoy some fun from time to time. If we put money aside every month for our personal enjoyment, we may be impressed how much more productive we would

become and how much more loved we would feel. Don't make a habit of taking care of everybody else and ignoring yourself. You're a queen and you deserve some constant tender loving care from you to yourself. It's your way of thanking yourself for all the work you do and for simply being this awesome and ensuring that you stay awesome forever. Self care has to be deliberate and we must not wait until we start earning higher to begin to make room in our budget for self care, it must not always be the most expensive things but can be as simple as an ice-cream treat or taking a trip to a relaxing beach or art gallery that we love or simply going to the salon for a manicure or pedicure or change of hairstyle. Little by little, once we start and begin to enjoy the rewards of self-care, we would be encouraged to do more and even to splurge on ourselves better when our income finally increases as we hope. If we don't start now, we just might never ever start even when we become millionaires because there will always be bills to pay as our income increases. As we grow in our finances, our allocation for self-care may naturally increase so that we begin to afford more options of fun and entertainment. These can include gym memberships, Netflix subscriptions, movie tickets, karaoke, Spa visits, restaurant outings and Vacations etc.

6. FAITH, CHARITY AND CELEBRATIONS: This is fund we set aside to spend on supporting friends and family, during their downtime or in moments of celebrations like to give gifts during birthdays, weddings, graduations, etc. From this, we may also support people who we desire to help everyday as well as make faith-based donations and any such obligations like association or club dues. Once this money finishes, then relax knowing you have done your best and you can move any more requests for help to the next batch of income you receive. Giving can be so satisfying. Ensure that you give out of love and the genuine kindness of your heart, never out of compulsion. There are people who are experts at guilt-tripping and roping

someone into unplanned expenses often with incessant and manipulative pleas. It is important to apply logic and know when you have exhausted your budget for faith, charity, and celebrations for the month so that you don't get into debts trying to help others, especially those who form a habit of pushing you over your budget all the time. You can help yourself and even more people in the long run if you attain a higher level of financial independence by sticking to your budget. So stay focused now and don't let your kindness be a hindrance to your financial progress. It is not always very easy but we can try.

7. EMERGENCIES: This is for unforeseen emergencies and things we probably never even thought could happen. Medical emergencies, Insurance and debt payments fit in here as well.

Creating a Personalized Budget

Everybody's budget will not look the same, but will be a reflection of their immediate needs, priorities and future aspirations. Senator Elizabeth Warren brought popularity to the "50/20/30 budget rule in her book, All Your Worth: The Ultimate Lifetime Money Plan. This rule suggests that we divide up after-tax income and allocate it to spend: 50% on needs, 30% on wants, and save 20% for rainy days and investments. There are many different variations of the budget rule because everybody's needs, wants and future aspirations differ in the short term and in the long run depending on a lot of factors. So I have created 3 likely sample budget plans for different women, being careful to reflect their situations in life. It is my hope that this will give us a well rounded appreciation for budgets so we can go ahead to plan ours.

Sample 1

Name: Laura

Age: 21

Job: Information Marketing

Background: Laura is a single lady who lives in the city with her wealthy parents. She values friendship, as well as her career. She is dating her high-school sweetheart who doesn't want to get a job and depends on her. She has some financial intelligence as she started investing from an early age. Romance is her Achilles' heel.

Savings: 10%

Investment: 20%

Recurrent expenses: 10%

Faith, Gifts, Celebrations: 35%

Personal development: 15%

Self Care: 10%

Emergencies: 0%

Sample 2

Name: Clara

Age: 32

Job: Cleaner and Clerk

Background: Clara is a widow who lives with her 3 children in the suburbs. She has adopted a victim mindset that makes it difficult for her to position herself for better opportunities around her. The bulk of her income goes to buying what her children want, sometimes at the expense of their basic needs. She enjoys a loving relationship with her parents who she moved closer home to take care of. She inherited her late husband's poultry business which funds her children's education and her secret hobby.

Savings: 0%

Investment: 10%

Recurrent expenses: 60%

Faith, Gifts, Celebrations: 10%

Personal development: 5%

Self Care: 10%

Emergencies: 5%

Sample 3

Name: Amara

Age: 37

Job: Bank Executive

Background: Amara is a married woman with twin boys and 2 girls. She lives and works in a different city from her husband and children. She is an avid reader and enjoys fun time with her girlfriends. She contributes to her family finances and is determined not to suffer the same financial lack she believes her parents did, so she buries herself in climbing the corporate ladder as fast as she can. She hopes to be able to invest enough so she can afford to live closer to her loved ones someday.

Savings: 10%

Investment: 25%

Recurrent expenses: 35%

Faith, Gifts, Celebrations: 10%

Personal development: 10%

Self Care: 5%

Emergencies: 5%

These three women are just like you and I. Their financial decisions are driven by their perceptions and predicaments. We may be able to get a glimpse into their quality of life both now and in the future. While it is important to apply financial intelligence on the road to financial freedom, it is even more important to enjoy a life where our needs are met and we still have enough time to enjoy life with the ones we love. This necessitates an appropriate balance between time and money.

After we decide how best to plot our budget based on the things that are most important to us at a particular time bearing in mind our vision and goals for that period and in the long run, we can now start looking for ways to ensure that the cash and other resources we need are available to us. Let us look at Time and Money, and the role they play in the quality of holistic living we access as women.

8.3 TIME

"Not everything that can be counted counts, and not everything that counts can be counted."

This quote is often attributed to Albert Einstein but is more likely gotten from the book Informal Sociology: a casual introduction to sociological thinking written by Sociologist William Bruce Cameron.

In understanding the true role of time in the personal economics of our lives, let us look at the full statement thus;

"It would be nice if all of the data which sociologists require could be enumerated because then we could run them through IBM machines and draw charts as the economists do. However, not everything that can be counted counts, and not everything that counts can be counted."

Time is such an interesting resource and can be quite elusive. The beauty of time is that time well spent can yield more money. But I fear that we may never be able to buy time lost even with more money.

So this has led me to the conclusion that in our daily living as women, we must put the things that really matter into focus at all times. **How you choose to spend your time matters, even more than how you spend your money.** If you continue to deny your body sleep and adequate rest because you are chasing money, your body will betray you in the future just as you betray it in the present. If you sacrifice relationships that matter today in the pursuit of money, you may find that when you have all the money, the money is unable to buy you the time lost and even the loyalty of the people you pushed aside in your pursuit for money. Also, if you are sidelined by your relationships and present desires that you fail to make sound financial choices that gives you more passive income tomorrow, you may also find that you do not have enough money in future to truly retire and enjoy life with the people you love and in the ways you love.

So, it may be wise, to find a middle ground between these two key resources, Time and Money. We will look at contentment and delayed gratification, two ways to stay in the middle ground. First, let us look at some ways to increase our time and money resources.

More Time, More Money!

We all desire more time and more money to live the life we have always dreamed of. To have a life where we can focus on our nutrition, exercise, work, rest and relaxation, as well as enjoy relationships that matter is absolutely possible irrespective of age and financial status. Well, here are a few things that the modern woman who wishes to win in the game of holistic living can do to increase her time and money to enjoy her best life.

1. CAPACITY DEVELOPMENT

If we commit to improving ourselves regularly, we will find that we become better. As we improve on our ability to love and serve, as well as lead and create, we begin to attract better opportunities in our everyday relationships and finances. So whether you're single or married, continue to attend trainings, conferences, read books etc in line with your life goals. Leverage on your new and improved capacity to access more money and time, at work, at home, and in your personal life.

2. PORTFOLIO CAREER

A portfolio career is simply a way to monetize our skills in several different ways that our time can yield more money from multiple sources at the same time. It is often referred to as having multiple streams of income or in my Nigerian lingua, **side hustles**.

Many times we fear the ridicule of others and allow it as an excuse not to pursue a portfolio career. Many naysayers abuse the adage Jack of all Trades, master of none, and use it to hinder the expression of those who are multi-talented. But it is only if you allow them deter you from the big picture. In truth, the original saying goes thus, **"A jack of all trades is a master of none, but oftentimes better than a master of one."** When you look at the full saying, you realize it was intended as a compliment and not as a tool for ridicule. We should pursue multiple expressions if we are so gifted, because that is what it means to be resourceful. Not everybody has multiple competencies because sometimes we ignore our raw talents but some people hone their talents and skills in a way that it yields them money. So, over time, they become masters of several things. If you are one of such people, then embrace this treasure within you.

Freelancing is a great way to pursue a portfolio career and offer the same services to several companies and organizations at the same time. I had the privilege of embarking on the journey of self-discovery as a teenage girl and so I have gone on to maximize my many talents to become an effective Jack of many trades, and master of some. I have diversified into different fields that interest me, taking a step further to build systems and structures around them in a way that has given birth to businesses with varying degrees of income and satisfaction.

However, we need to minimize the risk of being overwhelmed and eventual burnout even as we pursue a portfolio career. Taking life one day at a time.

3. SOCIAL CAPITAL

Social capital is all about relationships and networks. Show love to the people around you. Open your heart to forgive yourself and forgive others and in so doing, you will be able to show love and build meaningful relationships that matter, both in the long run and now.

Our social capital is a goldmine that will make up for so much else we may lack by way of Time and Money. We can start a new business or advance in our career if we have goodwill and even when we don't have money, colleagues, friends and family may be willing to lend us a helping hand for that forward push.

Learn to ask for help as often as you need it and be willing to receive it from the people that love you when they offer it. Delegate where the need arises to create more time for you to do other things. We talked about delegation as a key ingredient for effective Work in Chapter 4 of this book.

4. INVESTMENTS

Investing will help us create more time. When we invest we are taking money from today and putting it into something that will yield income later on. ***The money we invest today can buy us more free time tomorrow to do the things we love.*** It is making our money work for us, instead of working for money.

DELAYED GRATIFICATION & CONTENTMENT

When I relocated to Lagos towards my wedding time to plan it, I stayed with my elder sister who graciously helped me secure a job. I had moved from my own apartment and private office that was right in the heart of the city of Enugu, directly opposite the home of the then Deputy President of the Nigerian Senate. I had moved out of my parent's house and rented that space with a bulk of my savings after I returned from Anambra state where I had managed a radio station. My job as a Station manager had come with a fully furnished 2 bedroom apartment and I had grown accustomed to the luxury of privacy. So when I moved back home, I preferred to start my own life and rent an apartment where it pleased me, with little consideration for the future financial impact. I loved the luxury of privacy.

So when I had to lock my sweet and private apartment and move to Lagos, I figured it was just a matter of time before my wedding and I would get a chance to select a cozy apartment in my choice part of the city to call my matrimonial home. I proceeded to share my excitement and plans with my husband-to-be who burst my bubbles.

Imagine my shock and tears when he told me we wouldn't be moving to my preferred part of town till we could afford to. Firstly, there was a housing crisis in the state because of the population issue common to most metropolis and so housing was unusually exorbitant, beyond my wildest expectations. In comparison, my experience of rent in my former city and in this new one was like comparing the speed of a butterfly to an airplane.

Even at that, it was still tough accepting that we could not afford where I had wanted us to live even though I could clearly see that we could make the rent between us. I had a hard time wrapping my head around it because that was not how I approached my finances. If I had money for something, I would simply do it, whether or not it was sustainable or detrimental to my financial health in the long run. He explained that if we were to live in a place that takes up a bulk of our income, we would struggle to enjoy other niceties like a weekend getaway, or even making investments. We may live in a cozy neighborhood, but may struggle with the other things that matter to us as a new couple such as spending Sundays together. We could move to an expensive neighborhood and spend the next few years working ourselves too hard to meet our expenses, or we could live in a neighborhood we could truly afford and create a plan to invest parts of our income so that one day, we can own a home wherever we wanted.

Understanding his perspective was a great turning point in my approach to my finances and has often helped me place my financial priorities right per time ever since. There are still days when I throw all caution away and just do whatever I feel like doing with my money, but for the most part, I am more prudent and have come to enjoy some level of success in my personal finances as I implement this strategy.

And it is this same recommendation that I offer as a way to balance our time and money both in the short and long run.

Contentment and delayed gratification may be the middle ground to ensure that we are not being complacent in the management of our finances and time today, even as we seek to maximize our everyday life and enjoy financial freedom in the future.

Delaying gratification is simply holding off on something you want today for a much preferred future. It is what happens when you plant a seed to yield even much more today instead of eating the seed today and having to struggle for more seed to eat when tomorrow comes.

> ***Contentment is being satisfied with what you have, no matter what anyone else has. It is simply a state of being enough.***

The fact that you can doesn't always mean that you should. You can work 3 jobs but should you? Would working 3 jobs allow you enough time to take care of your own self and enjoy the relationships that matter to you? It may give you more money but may rob you of your time. And if you make an investment, then perhaps you should be strategic about it, being careful to do it in a way that you are at a place where your needs are met in the present as well as in future, and these include physical, mental, emotional and spiritual needs. Do not form the habit of investing the money for your immediate bread and go hungry just because you seek financial independence. Take care of your basic needs, please, even in your bid to invest. There is no point in sacrificing today for the promise of tomorrow but at the same time, do not squander your tomorrow in the enjoyment of today.

Some ways we can practice contentment and delayed gratification include;

1. Being deliberate about taking breaks and being honest with ourselves on what we can and cannot do per time.

2. Living below our means. It is difficult to resist the temptation of buying the most luxurious products and services but we just have to try our best to keep our eyes on the ball and focus on our vision board. Once our needs are met, wants are secondary and we'll be just fine eventually.

3. Downsizing. We reduce our excesses if it will help our finances in the long term. We can consider moving to a more affordable neighborhood so we can have more money to invest instead of putting the bulk of our income into rent and being left with nothing much to invest towards our future.

4. Minimizing debt. Let's do our best to resist the lure of debt. If we don't form the habit of being in debt for our personal finances, we are more likely to learn how to live below our means eventually.

5. Avoiding comparisons. We may not ever be truly happy if we continue to compare ourselves to other people who have different backgrounds, strengths and future. Comparisons will rob you of your joy and sleep and push

you into making stupid decisions that add very little value to your life. An entitlement mindset and a victim mindset are usually the culprits whenever there is comparison present. Somehow we feel that we deserve what another person has or that life is unfair to us and that is why we do not have the same opportunities that others have. Let us shake off those mindsets because they can rob our peace and joy and may even push us into sadness or depression. Let's concentrate on our own victories and be patient with ourselves and our vision.

5. Being grateful. Gratitude is such a powerful force. If you are grateful for what you have, you are content. **Say thank you when people help you, understanding they don't owe you the help.** Ultimately, be grateful to God for the gift of life because at every point in life, we are winning whether we realize it or not. We all came into this life naked and with nothing, so whatever little we own today, even if it is just the bra on our chest, is one thing more than we had when we came in to this life.

Content makes poor men rich. Discontent
makes rich men poor.
- BENJAMIN FRANKLIN

CHAPTER 9
CONCLUSION

In the past 12 years of my career as an event host, there is always that one person who walks up to me at the end of the event to compliment me and remark how wonderful my hosting skills are.

I would often smile and thank them and sometimes we exchange business cards.

Deep within, I smile to think of every road that has led me here. It has been years of practice, showing up in good and bad weather, lots of training and mentorship, failing and getting back up, putting on a brave face on the scariest days, many days seeking God's face and a lot of personal sacrifice and commitment. When we judiciously pour 12 years of our life into a particular endeavor, we're bound to stand out.

Here's one encounter that was instrumental in the confidence that I exude off and on the stage of life. The year was 2012 and I had traveled to the city of Enugu for a comedy show I was slated to perform in. Yes, I started out as a stand up comedienne, which was what birthed event hosting for me. As was often the case, I was the only female comedian for the night. I was sure I would *break a leg*.

Plot twist; the show was coming to an end and the event compere had still not called me to the stage. I turned to my then manager with panic in my eyes when people started to leave around 8pm. The mic wasn't hot anymore, every one of the male comedians had performed and the show was seen to be over. I was blushing with embarrassment because David had told me I had a sure slot on the show, seeing as at the time I had already traveled abroad as part of a comedy tour and even toured Nigeria with some prominent comedians with my face all over posters and billboards. You can imagine my disappointment at that treatment in my own city.

David proceeded to do one thing that has come to make a lot of difference in my career. He convinced me to get on that stage and perform to an almost empty hall. He said *paraphrased*, "Olivia, if you get on that stage and perform to even just one person who cares to listen, you will have built the confidence it takes to perform to thousands. But even if you don't find one person, perform for the camera, because you never know where this video will get to someday."

His words propelled me to get on that stage and as I began to perform, the most beautiful thing happened. The people who were already leaving started to laugh and then they began to turn around to see who was on stage. Even the people who were already in the parking lot were coming back into the hall to watch me perform. And then almost like in a movie, everybody started going back to their seats. By the time I was done, everyone was reeling with laughter and I got an overwhelming ovation from the audience. It was such a wonderful feeling, and I just had to hold myself from bursting into sweet tears. I had never seen anything quite like the audience reaction that night and I didn't even think I was that funny back then.

Two things I'll never forget from that wonderful night; the extreme chill from the cold, I did not carry a jacket as I didn't realize it would be an outdoor event on such a chilly night and the excitement on people's faces when they heard the only female comedian performing for the night.

One thing was settled that night;

Every time I get on any stage today, I know that it can't get worse than performing to an almost empty hall. I had faced one of my worst nightmares and overcome it.

David was absolutely right. After that day, there has never been any stage or audience too big or small for me, whether an intimate Master Class with just 10 participants or a roaring concert of 10 thousand fans. I have gone on to host weddings, conferences, seminars, pageants, panel sessions, cosplays, religious conferences, reunions, festivals etc, far bigger than that young comedienne could have imagined. And I've had billionaires like Madam Folorunsho Alakija, one of Africa's richest women and prominent heads of states as clients. But no matter where I go and what I do, I will never forget the young lady with sweaty palms in that auditorium and her bravery continues to inspire me. Win or lose, I have a feeling that I will always be fine at the end of the day and that is a comforting feeling.

What is your story of bravery? What lesson has your life taught you? And what are you most proud of in yourself? Let it be a guiding force in moments of doubt and let it strengthen you in moments of weakness, reminding you that irrespective of what is going on around you at all times, you are still that person who did those little big things. **It is okay to be afraid sometimes, but push through the fear with the force that is within you.** Always remember who you are.

So far, so good.

Writing this book has been a long road paved with so many raw emotions, and sprinkled with the joys and concerns that surround us as modern woman. I have been challenged by the many things discussed in this book, even to strive to do better myself. On this journey, we have explored the perceptions that drive us as women and done our very best to unravel the inspirations behind our everyday decisions and experiences. We have considered what truly inspires the choices we make when we choose what we eat every day, how we spend our time and money, and which relationships we pursue. Deep within us we are responding to our understanding of our own selves and our identity.

We found that if we truly relax and enjoy a restful time from all work, we give our body a much needed reward for its noble role in keeping up with the multiple functions it is tasked with daily and a chance to heal itself. And when we eat right and exercise, we can help boost our physical and mental health to enable us function in our daily work.

As women, it has become more important that we uphold the relationships that form a part of our history, our present and our future. And this is because we live in a technology age where organic human relationships have been on a decline and the mental health and emotions of many women is on a roller coaster ride. We find that after all is said and done, we cannot deny that we all need the love and care of our family, friends and loved ones to navigate our daily lives. You may be able to succeed alone, but you do not necessarily need to go through the rumored lonely path on your way to the top. Stop and smell the roses, and be intentional about reaching out and staying connected to the people you care about. If you do not have friends, then go ahead and make some today, firstly presenting yourself as a friend. Thankfully we discussed how to do that in details in chapter 6. Life is too short not to enjoy the beauty that relationships and friendships present. Yes, it can get lonely as we go up in life, but a friendly call from our mother here, a surprise visit from our girlfriend or even the reassuring hug from our lover or child can cushion this effect and help us enjoy a life that is filled with joy, laughter and beautiful stories, at whatever level we find ourselves on the ladder of success.

Brace yourself for the occasional heartbreaks that come from family and friends, and consider it a small price to pay for the privilege of sharing in the life of others. And learn to forgive yourself and others as quickly as the need arises. We all need each other, so let us make room for our own humanity and imperfections. It is wonderful to see the possibilities present when we let go our expectations of perfection in our relationship with ourselves and with others. I am not perfect and neither are you. It is a fact of life, and it is one of the things that make us desire a relationship with one another. Keep this in mind the next time you are hurting and let go easily. But love yourself enough to walk away from toxic relationships that seek only to take advantage of you and give nothing in return.

A woman who refuses to be treated less than she deserves, understands her worth and is not afraid to ask for that and more. The failure of society today is a failure of the family system. ***Women who are broken, mostly in their formative years, end up silenced and humbled into a place of toxic tolerance.*** We wonder how a woman stays in an abusive relationship; we now see that perhaps she cannot stand her own thoughts in the privacy of her own mind. So she runs away from her own self, and feels safer in the arms of an external tormentor, rather than sit still and alone for a few minutes for fear of the torment that rages within her own soul. ***Women who are broken inside will stay with anybody but themselves irrespective of the abuse.*** For them, to be alone, is to be utterly lonely and miserable. So, as women, we must seek to find fulfillment in our own lives so that we continue to demand the love and respect that we deserve in every relationship we find ourselves.

Do the things that make you happy and leave you breathless. This includes exercise and sex with your spouse.

There are many benefits of indulging in wholesome sex with your spouse once you are married and committed to each other, so do not form a habit of denying yourself these benefits. Take off the cloak of shyness and come fully into your sensual potentials as a woman. And even when you become a mother, follow the guidelines outlined in this book to bring the spark back into your bedroom.

Watch Out!

There are some people that will try to put you down for no reason. These sets of individuals will try to convince you that what you've set your heart to do is not good enough. They'll assure you that it is unrealistic and far-fetched and you should not waste your time chasing shadows. They may say things like, what do you hope to gain by reuniting with your loved ones? They will only hurt you again! Or they may declare, why do you deceive yourself trying to lose weight by taking walks, can't you see that you will never lose weight ever? Or what do you mean that you are going back to school at your age? It is too late to pursue a new career path.

Sadly, they may be the people who we have looked up to our entire life and who we had hoped would applaud our desire for holistic living. Let me tell you, do not pay these people any attention. Watch out for such people and mind how you listen to them. I have encountered many naysayers who have done everything in their power to ridicule my best efforts at self improvement and derail me. But with time, I learnt to shut out the voice of negativity and concentrate on my inner voice. Especially after I discovered one amazing thing about these sets of people, which is that they'll go right ahead to do the same thing they tried to discourage us from if they get the chance. So we must never give them the pleasure of derailing us. Once you set your heart on a goal, fill your mind with thoughts of your vision and look at the vision board you created within you and in your immediate environment. Let it fuel your drive and shut out every voice of doubt. Daily affirm your convictions and your vision and always remind yourself who you are and why you have chosen the path you're on.

Anything you want to be…BE.

Anything you want to do…DO.

Don't even let someone who has gone ahead of you discourage you. Don't let them block your way and discourage you with tales of how difficult the journey to your destination is. If they could do it, you too can.

The sure way to succeed is to start. We can start small, start today, and start with what we have. We can make mistakes, learn from them and start again. Whatever we do, we can quit procrastinating and waiting for everything to be perfect. If you desire to take charge of your finances, or plant a garden, or write a book, or quit a bad habit or take a break or begin a relationship with God, **Just START**. Everything is possible to you. I am here to encourage you, one woman to another and to say, Just Start!

Woman; an Endangered Specie

One of the best things you can do for yourself as a woman is to start investing in your self-development early. Learn marketable skills and find meaningful ways to engage yourself. Once you realize that you can make an honest living through the works of your hands, it will be easier to identify and resist the temptation of unwholesome relationships and any path that doesn't align with your dreams, vision and purpose. We live in a society that targets women to lay waste to their future with the promise of easy wealth and a lavish lifestyle. If we can catch a vision for our life and stay focused on our path, it is easy to run with this vision forever. We are better served pursuing jobs and relationships that align with our dreams than ones that are necessitated by lack.

Don't allow yourself to be distracted by society's objectification of the body of a woman, dictating how she should look and even what shade she must be. Don't allow anybody to reduce your worth to the size of your body parts or the brightness of your skin color, causing you to bleach and harm yourself in unthinkable ways as you seek to conform to ever-changing standards and illusions. All these are simply battles of the mind, so we have to condition our mind to think beyond society's dictates and shake off every limitation that has held us down before now. As my husband would often say, **you are the biggest hero in your own life story.**

I write for the women who feel that their beauty is a commodity that must be explored in exchange for money and favors or a handicap because she believes society won't take her serious because she's too beautiful. Do not run and hide because of the bad experiences you have been through. And do not be distracted by your own beauty, because beauty may fade as you age but your value is inside of you, not tied to your beauty, and never fading. It is time to stop running, stand and challenge whatever has stood in your path to holistic living. Tear down every imagination and stronghold that has laid siege in your mind and limited you in the past.

Don't let society define you or constrain you to their box of vanity. It's time to get angry. If all people see about you is your straight legs, **Get Angry**. If all they ever compliment is your gorgeous curves, **Get Furious**. Rise up and do something. Change something. Keep learning and investing in your self-development until they start to see you for who you truly are.

A true visionary. Master Innovator. An embodiment of life and virtue. A happy soul.

One day, you can bring change that will cause lasting impact. But it will be on your own terms. You do not owe it to anybody to prove anything. You will be respected for what value you bring to the table. You can and you will become a force to be reckoned with. Can you envision it? See yourself having a seat at the UN, being listed in Forbes 30 under 30, becoming a world champion at the Olympics, an agent for social change, a loving mother, a happy wife, a humanitarian. Or simply woman. Whatever you choose, you can be. And you are ENOUGH.

The Holistic Woman!

I know that the world calls us super women sometimes and we bask in the glory of being seen. But between us, we must always keep in mind that we are only human, and admit that even on our best days, we are flesh, blood, memories and hope. So let us always be kind to our own selves. Let us remember to laugh at our mistakes and learn from them but do our best to move on quickly and continue to live our best lives. ***Do not be so taken by the promise of a better future that you forget to enjoy what it means to be present in the experiences of today, no matter how they may be.*** Open your eyes wide and enjoy all the experiences that have brought you where you are today. Celebrate every little win, whether it is winning an award at work or simply getting out of bed in the morning.

Everything that has happened so far in our lives has brought us to this moment, where we choose our own happiness and make moves to honor our own selves by living a deliberate and holistic lifestyle. May we soar together on this beautiful journey of Womanhood.

Cheers to our mutual health and wellness and a life filled with so many beautiful memories.

To physical, and mental health and wellness.

To beautiful friendships and adventure,

To love and romance,

To a happy-ever-after.

Cheers, to becoming a holistic woman.

REFFERENCES

Bill Gates. 1999. *Business At The Speed of Thought*. Business Plus. New York.

Derek Llewellyn-Jones. 1971. *Every Woman*. Faber and Faber Limited. London.

Dr. Emerson Eggerichs. 2004. *Love and Respect*. Thomas Nelson Inc. Nashville.

Josh McDowell, Bob Hostetler. 1996. Josh McDowell's Handbook on Counseling Youth. Thomas Nelson. Nashville.

Robert T. Kiyosaki, Sharon L. Lechter. 1999. *Cashflow Quadrant*. Warner Business Books. New York.

Tim LaHaye. 1994. *Spirit Controlled Temperament*. Tyndale House Publishers Inc. Illinois.

T. Scot Gross. 1995. *How To Get What You Want From Almost Everybody*. Health Communications Inc. Florida.

This book guides the modern woman through a deliberate journey of achieving a wholesome personality on all sides. From the state of your mental well being to factors that strengthen the physical, spiritual, emotional, financial and social health of a holistic woman. It is in the elements of the thoughts we entertain, the choice of food we eat, the exercise we engage in, the quality of rest and relaxation we allow ourselves, the positive energy we harvest from the relationships we nurture around us, the deliberate and strategic thoughts we give to managing our financial resources, and most importantly, the wisdom with which we handle the subject of our spirituality. Olivia addresses all these from both personal experiences and proven scientific reports.

After reading this book, the reader would be better empowered to tackle disturbing issues like unstable relationships, poor self-esteem, depression, physical health challenges, financial weaknesses, eating disorders, etc., all arising from the heavy demands on the modern day woman to meet up to society's domestic, social, economical, parental and religious obligations.

ABOUT THE AUTHOR

Olivia Uchechukwu, popularly known as McOlivia is a seasoned media professional with over 12 years experience in TV and radio presenting, production, event MC and content creation. She started out as a teenage standup comedy sensation and have gone on to build a formidable media career working with several multinational brands.

McOlivia has hosted over 100 high profile events ranging from corporate dinners, conferences, awards, VIP red carpets, weddings and more. She also runs several businesses which include McOlivia's Kitchen and an NGO, McOlivia Foundation.

Her journey through womanhood and motherhood while navigating the demands of career and entrepreneurship pushes her to contemplate and explore the secrets of balancing life as a woman. She currently lives in Lagos with her husband and daughter.